A Modern Approach to

BASKETRY

with Fibers and Grasses

A Modern Approach to

BASKETRY

with Fibers and Grasses

USING COILING · TWINING ·
WEAVING · MACRAMÉ ·
CROCHETING

BY DONA Z. MEILACH

CROWN PUBLISHERS INC. NEW YORK

Inquiries should be addressed to Crown Publishers, Inc.
419 Park Avenue South, New York, N.Y. 10016

Library of Congress Catalog Card Number: 74-77482
Printed in the United States of America
Published simultaneously in Canada by
General Publishing Company Limited
Designed by Shari de Miskey and Kendra McKenzie

Contents

Acknowledgments

Delving into basketry and the people involved with the new visions and creativity it heralds has been a wild, wonderful experience. Baskets are relatively small and hard to damage, so the majority of pieces illustrated throughout the book were shipped or brought to me to be photographed. My primary indebtedness goes to the hundreds of artist-craftsmen who created, packed, and sent the pieces. Each person's name accompanies his examples. I am grateful to the efficiency and reliability of United Parcel Service, which never damaged or delayed a single piece.

A special vote of thanks goes to Kathy Malec, Park Ridge, Illinois, who developed many of the procedures while I photographed them and who helped me laugh away an entire day's work wasted because of a nonfunctioning camera.

Words alone can't convey my thanks to Joan Sterrenburg and Budd Stalnaker of Indiana University's Department of Fine Arts, Bloomington, Indiana. They asked their current and past weaving students to bring back the baskets that had been created for special assignments. I spent three days photographing the pieces and as a house guest of the Sterrenburgs. Many of these students have since become teachers at various colleges throughout the country, and, wherever you are now, thank you.

My gratitude to Joan Austin, San Diego State University, California, who nurtured my awareness of the growing activity in basketry and showed me the basic principles involved.

I am indebted to the enthusiasm of Lillian Donald, Pasadena City College, California, who suggested that her students ship their work to me. It was thrilling to see how her inspired teaching stimulated so many outstanding examples. Among them are Molly Barross's twined baskets that were the essence of her master's degree thesis and which she sent to me to study.

Thank you, Eileen Bernard, Reseda, California, for spending a weekend at my home and holding an informal seminar with ten Chicago area weavers. Your experience with coiling techniques established several of the easy-to-perform methods and shortcuts demonstrated in the chapter on coiling.

vii

This book could never have been realized without the complete cooperation of my husband, Dr. Melvin M. Meilach. He offers encouragement and solace when the mountain of material seems as if it will never fall into an organized, cohesive book. He assists with the photography and pitches in as associate shipping clerk on a kitchen table covered with boxes, wrappings, and rope instead of meals.

My thanks to my typist, Marilyn Regula, and to Ben Lavitt, of Astra Photo Service, Incorporated, Chicago, for his good-natured handling of my photographic processing demands.

I am indebted to my editor, Brandt Aymar, and to Crown Publishers, who have the ability to anticipate the need for a book on a hitherto untouched subject, who give me a free hand as to its content and design, and then bring it to completion efficiently and beautifully.

Dona Z. Meilach
Palos Heights, Illinois

Note: All photos by Dona and Mel Meilach unless otherwise credited.

Foreword

Contemporary basketry could be likened to the awakening of a sleeping giant. Baskets and basketry techniques are almost as ancient as man himself. Yet, they are so new that many experienced crafts people are unaware of the renaissance occurring in basketry. Those who are studying the ancient techniques and adapting them to modern arts are quick to admit that they are just beginning to touch upon and explore the potential they promise.

A Modern Approach to Basketry with Fibers and Grasses deals with the use of coiling, twining, weaving, macramé, and crochet made with fibers and applied to containers, container forms, sculpture, and other areas of artistic expression. It also explores the application of traditional woods and grasses usually associated with the basketmaker's production for contemporary art statements. It charts a new course for discovery among the methods and materials used by our ancestors combined with the materials and thoughts of today.

The concept of modern craftsmen making baskets is still met with eyebrow-raising skepticism by the uninformed. A safe prediction is that this narrow vision will soon be as bombarded and as broken down as the atom. This book and the people who have contributed to it are the means by which it will be done.

It is an exciting prospect.

1

Basketry: A Modern Art Form

People working in the fiber arts are revising creative methods used centuries ago. It is not surprising that they are looking backward in time and accomplishment, studying the basketmaking techniques of primitive cultures and concluding that they contain untapped potential for contemporary expressive statements.

This is the same artistic climate that spurred weavers to take respite from mechanical looms and to rediscover off-loom and finger-weaving methods of the American Indians. Macramé, the ancient knotting technique popular with nineteenth-century sailors and old Arabic garment makers, continues to enjoy unprecedented popularity. Fiber sculptures and wall hangings have burst upon the art consciousness in such dimension that staid, conservative museum directors have dusted off their tradition-colored glasses to give them display space that normally was reserved for wood, metal, and stone sculptures.

In a few short years, fiber arts have become so respected that names of their artists are becoming as well known to curators, collectors, and the public as those of major painters and sculptors. As this respect increases, more and more artist-craftsmen are turning their attention to the statements that can be expressed through fibers. They are as intent on searching out additional ways to make this statement as the sculptor or painter is on seeking new stimulation for his creativity.

With this foundation, interest in basketry is bubbling and fermenting like a delicious brew. It began with a fever to collect baskets from many cultures because of their form, color, and pattern. Then, artists began to study the structure of baskets that are coiled, twined, and woven from natural materials. They began to explore the possibility of creating these structures, or similar ones, in new media.

Evidence indicates that the man who may have started it all is Ed Rossbach, an eminent teacher at the University of California at Berkeley. A collection of American Indian and Pre-Columbian basketry in the University's Department of Physical Anthropology was available to stu-

<

SEUSS BASKET. Gyyle Luohaaaa. Coiling English mohair with linen over a core of cotton roving.

Indian water-bottle basket. 9 inches high, 7-inch diameter. Twill weaving. Baskets that were made to hold water were usually tightly woven of a native grass that would expand when wet so the materials would tighten up and form a solid surface.
Collection, Stana Coleman
Evanston, Illinois

dents in the Department of Decorative Art. When Mr. Rossbach joined the department in 1952 (it was then the only university offering a Master of Fine Arts degree in weaving), he had already begun a series of researches into nonproduction, nonutilitarian fabric, and in the 1960s basketry techniques piqued his interest.

His approaches to teaching soon included the results of his studies and fired an enthusiasm in students such as Joan Austin and Joan Sterrenburg. These talented young women took college teaching posts where weaving was becoming a respected subject to study. Ms. Austin, who had been raised along the California coast, was familiar with fibers, ropes, and knots. A study of Pomo Indian baskets, coupled with her weaving training, fostered a pervasive thirst for learning about basket techniques from every culture. Her students at the University of Illinois, Champaign, Illinois, and San Diego State University, California, delved into basketry studies also.

Joan Sterrenburg brought her expertise to Indiana University, Bloomington, Indiana, where for the past several years she and weaver Budd Stalnaker have given assignments to students to create "containers" from fibers using basketry and other techniques. The results from these

Coiled basket. New Guinea. 7 inches high, 11 inches wide, 6-inch diameter.
*Collection, Joan Sterrenburg,
Bloomington, Indiana*

two wellsprings have been astounding. Their graduate students have assumed teaching posts and continue to teach basketry. It is growing in popularity so quickly that workshops and summer courses are being offered in arts and crafts programs in various parts of the country.

Exactly what is contemporary basketry? How does it differ today from the baskets we know so well and that have been produced for centuries?

Webster's definition is:

BASKETRY, the art of making baskets; work
consisting of plaited osiers or twigs.

With current activity in basketmaking, Webster will have to update that definition. Contemporary basketmakers are more often making baskets from fibers such as cotton, linen, wool, jute, and sisal, rather than willow, reed, cane, and grasses normally associated with the basketmaker's output. A thorough discussion of fibers and grasses and their contemporary usages is presented in Chapter 2.

Twining and coiling, two basic methods for beginning and working a basket, are illustrated in these ceremonial plaques made by Hopi Indians in the early twentieth century using native grasses. The identical methods are applied to contemporary baskets, which may employ grasses but more usually use fibers varying from fine weaving threads to heavy ropes. Left, twining technique (a weaving approach) begins with two twined squares overlaid and trussed together. Twining continues around all the spokes. Right, a coiled basket using the Figure Eight stitch.

Courtesy, Newark Museum,
Newark, New Jersey

A revised explanation of the word "basket" may also be addended to such current definitions in dictionaries and encyclopedias as:

BASKET, a container made by hand by
interlacing or coiling and sewing vegetable fibers
and used for carrying.

Contemporary baskets may be containers, or shaped like containers, but, unlike those created by early peoples, the modern craftsman does not rely on the baskets he makes for utilitarian purposes or for carrying anything. He can create baskets for the sheer joy of manipulating and giving birth to a form with materials he enjoys working with. He can draw from the rich background offered by past cultures, but he builds his concepts into a fluid, exciting, and contemporary work that is as divorced from its beginnings as the modern oven is from the open fireplace.

To understand the derivation of modern baskets, a historical and cultural survey of baskets is recommended. This book is not meant to offer

Three techniques are illustrated in these baskets made by the Menominee, Fraser, and Navaho Indians. At left, strips of leaves or grass are bundled and held together by thin pairs of twining cords. Decoration is added by stitching colored grasses on the top and in the braided handles. Center, a coiled basket has a definite color design. Right, a coiled basket with the wrapping, or weft, cords spaced so that the exposed core becomes part of the design.

Courtesy, Newark Museum,
Newark, New Jersey

a history of basketmaking; there are books surveying the basketry development of many cultures. One of the most comprehensive and yet to be improved upon is Otis T. Mason's *Aboriginal American Basketry,* published in 1902 and recently reissued under the title of *American Indian Basketry* (see Bibliography). A wealth of basketry ideas appear in art and anthropology books that deal with a specific country such as New Guinea, Egypt, Africa, Mexico, China, Tibet, Peru, and so forth. Examples can be found in encyclopedias under the entry "Basketry."

The best source of study for baskets is museum and private collections. Seeing a basket close up enables you to appreciate the sculptural form, the structural details, the materials, the decorations, and so forth.

Basketmaking is one of the oldest and most nearly universal crafts of primitive man. Yet it may never be possible for archaeologists to determine the antiquity and early distribution of the craft in some parts of the world because the vegetable fibers of which baskets are made are perishable. Nevertheless, numerous prehistoric examples have been preserved

Basketry techniques have been applied to forms other than baskets by different cultures. A model of a temple from the Fiji Islands combines braiding, wrapping, weaving, and lashing.

Courtesy, Field Museum of Natural
History, Chicago, Illinois

>

A cradle by Fraser River Indians is made of grasses probably over cane, using coiling and twill weaving. Strands are added to tie the infant into the basket. Handles are added elements that are utilitarian and decorative.

Courtesy, Newark Museum,
Newark, New Jersey

in arid dry caves, in tombs, and in other favorable environments in both spheres.

In the Americas, basketmaking developed before the potter's craft, and specimens have been found in Indian sites that have been radiocarbon-dated to a culture called Basket Maker, about 5000 B.C. Baskets discovered in Peru are believed to be at least five thousand years old. The first evidence of basketry in Europe appears about 2500 B.C. Radiocarbon of Egyptian artifacts yields a date of 3929 B.C. Apparent impressions of basket weaves were found in pottery of a late Neolithic Chinese culture of about 3000 B.C.

Hats fashioned by the Hupa Indians of the early twentieth century have the appearance and shaping of baskets. Vertical lines of twining using a Z twist, accomplished by compact twining, give the shape its texture. This is a simple variation of basic twining and is illustrated on page 149. Observe how the shape is expanded by the addition of extra spokes.

Courtesy, Newark Museum,
Newark, New Jersey

Mexican craftsmen brilliantly shape and work natural materials into figures. Left, the dress, shawl, and face are plain weaving; the basket is the twining technique. The musical instrument held by the figure at right is shaped by wrapping and shaping groups of strands.

Collection, Lori Kratovil, Cicero, Illinois

Rice Doll. Indonesia. Plain weaving and hand-carved very thin split wood are used for the ceremonial figure that is believed to ensure a good rice harvest.

Collection, Dona Meilach

Ceremonial Dance and Initiation Rite figure. New Guinea. Grass weft wrapped over a core of split wood provides the figure with the solidity and strength needed for its size.

Photo, Rubin Steinberg, taken at the
Jen Jacques Laurent Gallery, Papeete, Tahiti

Pomo Indian baskets are a constant and rich source of inspiration for the contemporary craftsman. The sizes range from very tiny, almost fingernail-size (*front center*) and graduate to the large canoe-shape basket shown. Shapes, colors, patterning techniques, and ornamental materials used by the Pomos are frequently emulated in a modern idiom.

Courtesy, Newark Museum,
Newark, New Jersey

All cultures, ancient as well as those of only a few generations ago, made baskets strictly for utilitarian purposes and for survival. Baskets were involved with a person's birth, life, and death. The baby was slung in a papoose frame or carried in a bassinet or cradle. At death a person's remains were carried, buried, or cremated in a mortuary basket.

During his lifetime man used basketry for matting in his bed, rugs on his floor, tables on which to set his food, awnings to protect him from the sun, and for a blanket under which he was married. Baskets were used to carry water, to cook food, to drink from, to fish with. They were essential in religious ceremonies, for carrying grain, and harvesting food. Chairs and toys were woven of basketry materials. When one thinks of the many uses of baskets and how long it took for their handweaving, it staggers the mind to contemplate the millions of hours spent, mostly by women, gathering and preparing the roots, branches, stems, and other parts of plants and working them patiently, tirelessly, into the necessary objects.

A bevy of beautiful, colorful baskets is still readily available in modern department and specialty stores. These are imported from Mexico, Taiwan, the Philippines, Italy, Japan, and other places and may be made of rattan and cane with wood bases or wire frames. They are all handwoven. So far, there has been no major mechanization of basketmaking

Three Pomo Indian baskets illustrate the use of leather, seashells, and exposed core coiling (the weft is spaced so the core material is exposed and creates pattern).

Courtesy, Newark Museum,
Newark, New Jersey

Eileen Bernard creates a modern adaptation of the Pomo basket using wool and raffia over a rope core and adding feathers and shells. 9 inches high, 8-inch diameter.

Baskets of the Haida, Aluet, and Yakutat Indians exhibit varied designs and open and closed weaves.

techniques with natural materials. These imported baskets are, neverthe-less, mass-produced and not the artistic product of the past nor the product of the innovative artist.

Perhaps both the demise of the lovingly made basket and the rise of the new artistic development can be credited to the plastics industry. Not too many years ago, manufactured plastic baskets began to appear everywhere; to hold bread on restaurant tables, to pack berries in at the supermarket, to carry our laundry and serve multiple uses. Plastic poured into molds or made into pressed impressions became an ugly and un-couth simulation of the beautiful baskets that were part of our heritage. There were countless exact replicas, each like the other. But they were functional, inexpensive, durable, and they flooded the market. There was no longer a need for basketmakers.

Now the need for beautiful functional baskets has disappeared and opened wide the doors for the artist to create forms that are frankly ex-pressive of his inner feelings; forms that are beautiful without the need of function; forms that give the creator the ability to explore his materials, to work with his hands, to feel with his soul and mind.

Perhaps the "why" of making baskets today is summed up in the above paragraphs. Craftsmen rebel against the plastic society, the mass-produced million-of-a-kind product. They seek to create individuality. At

The Japanese work with bamboo ingeniously. A grain scoop is woven from one half of the bamboo round, which has been split into wide and narrow strips. Wide strips become the warp; narrow weft strips are carried around and woven through, then lashed around the edge.

Collection, Dona Meilach

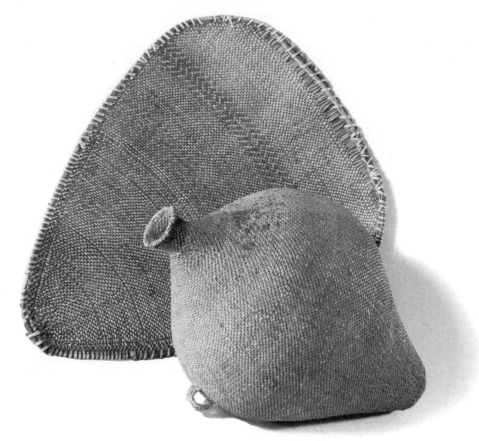

Water bottle and winnowing fan made by the Paiute Indians using the plain over-one, under-one weave.

Courtesy, Newark Museum,
Newark, New Jersey

the same time, there is a movement to go back to the earth, to explore another way of living than that offered by the tension-ridden, glittery facade of the big city. For some, creating a basket is the escape that offers the seclusion needed to think out the design, to work with the hands, to see a form evolve. No special materials are needed to make baskets, no complicated looms, no large work spaces. You and your materials alone are responsible for the outcome.

In a small booklet prepared by the Civic Arts Gallery of Walnut Creek, California, for a 1973 exhibition titled "Basketry," the exhibitors discuss why they make baskets. Nancy O'Banion talks about the tactile feeling of working with the materials and of "the constant pleasure of touching and smelling what I'm constructing."

Gyongy Laky, whose baskets include some made of plastics, ex-

Ethiopian basket. The Lazy Squaw stitch is used over coiled twigs for the cover and the bottom. A wide strip of wood forms the side of the basket. Negative spaces are accomplished with the solid twig core materials.

Photographed at the Anneberg Gallery,
San Francisco, California

plores the use of such materials, not as plastic, but as a construction material in the same way the Maori women use palms or the Africans use reeds. To her, the basket must stand on its own as sculpture. She creates forms that can stand, sit, or take a space and maintain it. Baskets need no ribs or other support, and if they are soft and fall a little that's fine. She can look at a small basket and think about how nice it would be if it were large enough to crawl into. And she has made some of her baskets just that large.

The reasons for creating baskets are as varied and as fascinating as the people who make them. It is sincerely hoped that you will feel the same way when you see the abundant and varied examples in the pages that follow.

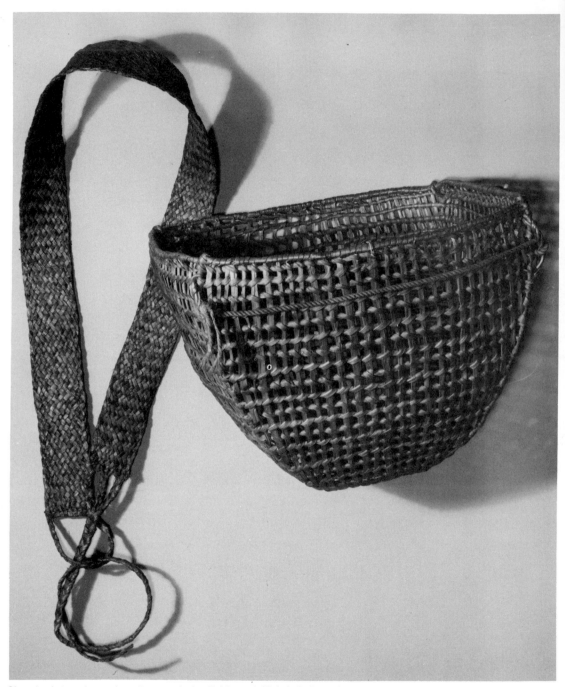

Clam basket and carrying strap made by Haida and Makah Indians (twentieth century). The basket is twined; the strap is finger-woven and braided.

Courtesy, Newark Museum,
Newark, New Jersey

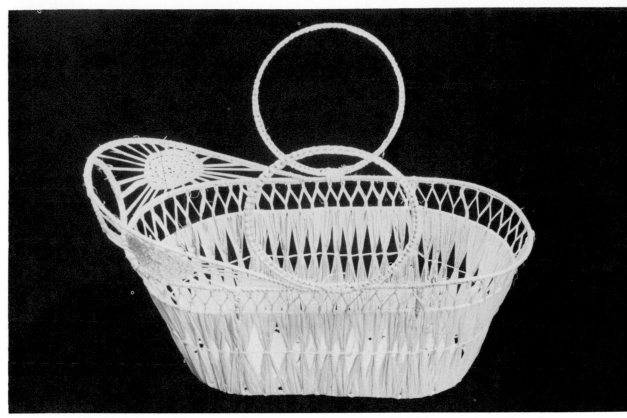

Wine basket. Italy. Contemporary. Grasses over a wire armature with twining, wrapping, and weaving.
Collection, Dona Meilach

Contemporary basket made in the People's Republic of China begins from a central Chinese Crown Knot (see p. 93) and continues in the twined technique. This same knot has been used for basket beginnings by American Indian tribes.

Collection, Dona Meilach

African exposed-core coiled basket. Wide strips of colored strawlike material are carried under and over the coils to form a surface design.

Collection, Stana Coleman, Evanston, Illinois

An Ethiopian coiled basket has an intricate design that differs on the inside and the outside. The edge is finished with strips of leather worked into the coiling.
Collection, Stana Coleman, Evanston, Illinois

Mexican craftsmen make a beaded basket of tiny, brilliantly colored beads set in beeswax. The designs can be applied to fiber baskets.
Private collection

The woven patterns in the straw baskets of the Cuna Indians are distinctive. They can be used for a basis for contemporary patterns in fiber baskets.
Collection, Stana Coleman, Evanston, Illinois

Bottom, left:
A woven basket from the Philippine Islands is made of caning. The basket is begun at the center bottom by crossing over grouped elements. The ends are disposed of by weaving them back toward the center within the rim.
Collection, Dona Meilach

Below:
Another coiling technique involves layering the coiled straws and gluing them together. An outside rib and a coiled foot are added for support. Waterproof glues must be used because the materials are usually shaped while damp. The finished basket should be able to withstand washing.
Collection, Dona Meilach

Antique decorative baskets are made from strips of ash and other woods, and combine many techniques and shapes.

Collection, Stewart Purinton, Oak Park, Illinois

CONTEMPORARY BASKETS

BASKET WITH BELLS. Kathy Woell. 5 inches high, 9½-inch diameter. Linen and wool yarn in the Lazy Squaw stitch over a twisted paper core. The added protrusions of linen and jute house small bells that jingle when the basket is moved. The small basket, 4 inches high, 5-inch diameter, is jute and linen with pheasant feathers. The Lazy Squaw stitch is also used in this basket.

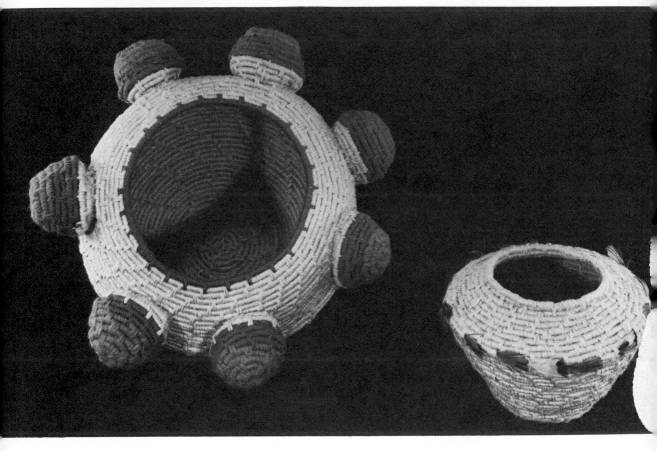

PINE-NEEDLE KNOTTED BASKET. Bonnie Zimmer. 8 inches high, 15-inch diameter. Dried pine needles form the core element for fibers worked in the Clove Hitch macramé knot. The pine needles protrude for the design concept and also take advantage of the nature of the material.

COILED BEIGE JUTE BASKET. Gary Trentham. 11 inches high, 7-inch diameter. Strands with knotted ends are added after the basket coiling is completed. The strands are pushed through the coils, then knotted and trimmed.

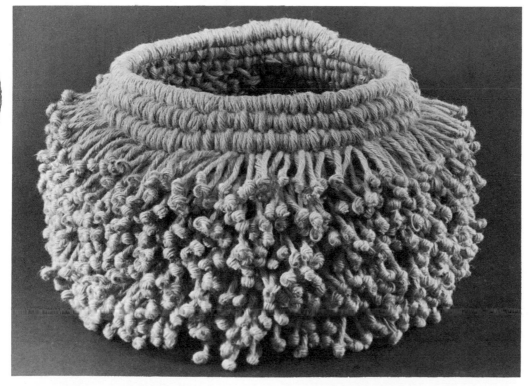

TISKIT. Louise Robbins. 10 inches high, 8 inches wide, 9 inches deep. Greek hand-spun wool and reeds. Lazy Squaw stitching with detached wrapped coils.

THREE CHIMNEYS. Marie Waters. 10 inches high, 5-inch diameter. Raffia and jute on raffia core with wooden beads at top. The three chimney shapes were made individually then assembled onto the base. The entire basket was dyed with walnut-hull dye after completion.

Courtesy, artist

GOURD BASKET. Steve Brixner. Lazy Squaw coiling attached to a gourd. Removable lid.

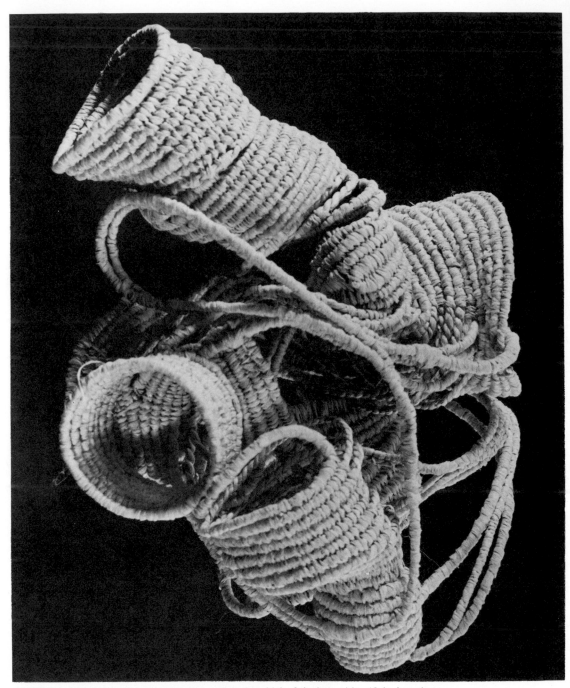

UNTITLED. Royce Zimon. In this position: 16 inches high, 9 inches wide, 12 inches deep. Free-form coiling with raffia over a raffia core. The piece can be set and viewed from several angles.

>

HANGING BASKET. Linda Ann Valeri. 14 inches high, 7-inch diameter. Coiled raffia with cock feathers, mink tails, and bamboo beads. Feathers protrude from an interior negative space and from the top.

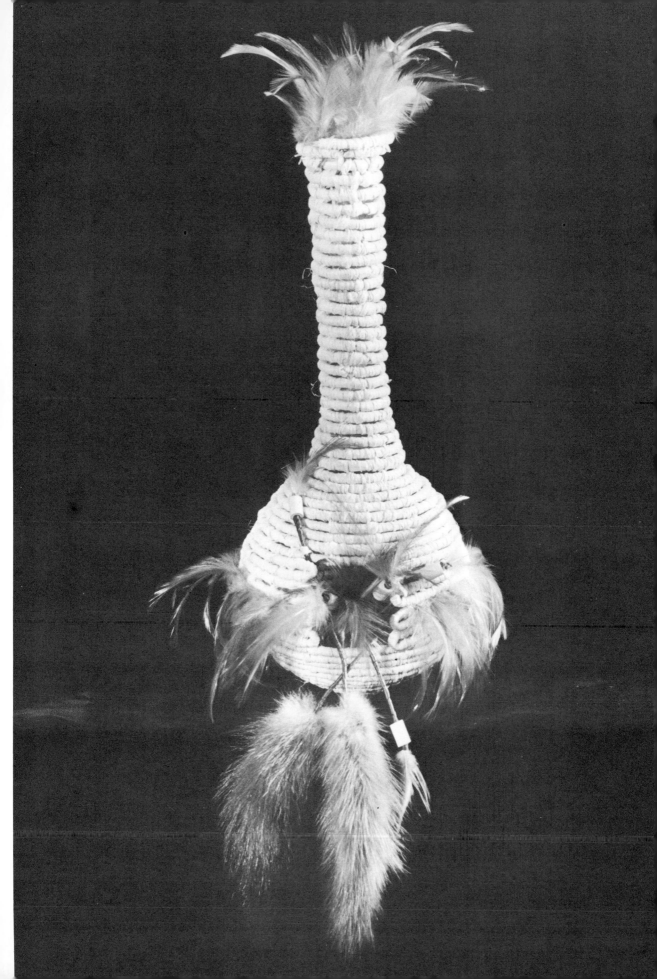

Materials for contemporary basketry include yarns and cords of various weights, textures, and fibers; wool, acrylics, jute, horsehair, goat hair, silk, linen, sisal, leather, sea grass, cane, willow reed, and others. Beads and feathers are natural decorative adjuncts. Wire, scissors, pliers, and an awl are essential for some procedures.

2

Materials

The materials that can be used for basketry are as varied as your imagination and experience can conjure. Ethnic peoples created baskets for utilitarian purposes and constructed them with natural woods and grasses indigenous to their regions. The contemporary artist has many more materials available to him, thanks to modern manufacturing processes and the import of fibers from all over the world. He can use natural materials as did our ancestors, but more likely he uses fibers or combines fibers with grasses for his artistic statement.

The contemporary basketmaker does not have to consider the basket's strength for carrying wood or coals, for holding a baby on one's back, or for catching fish, or whether it will hold water. His concern is with the basket as an art form and he can select his materials to serve that end. Neither does he have to worry about where his materials will come from or spend time harvesting and preparing them.

For clarity, we will refer to two kind of materials throughout the book: fibers and grasses.

Fibers are soft rope, twine, yarn, threads, roving, and so forth, spun and plied from silk, linen, jute, sisal, cotton, rayon, wool, and synthetic fibers. These are usually associated with weaving, knitting, macramé, and similar crafts. They are soft and pliable and almost always worked when they are dry.

Grasses will include hard materials normally used for traditional basketry and derived from small plants and trees. These are reed, willow, palm, sea grass, sedge, kelp, raffia, caning, split wood, wood splines, and others. They might be taken from roots, stems, bark, leaves, fruits, and gums. Such materials are not spun, as are fibers, and they are usually stiff or hard, and brittle. For pliability, many must be soaked in water before and while they are being worked.

Fibers and grasses, then, are the foundation of basketry. For some, no tools are needed; for others you may require a needle, wire, pliers, scissors, knives, and awls. Baskets may be colored with natural and synthetic dyes, and paints. They can be decorated with feathers, beads, bones, seashells, bells, and miscellaneous objects.

FIBERS

Almost every kind of fiber you can find can be worked into contemporary baskets. The criteria you employ will depend on the specific statement you have in mind, on the strength of the material, its texture, color, size, availability, and cost. It will depend on whether you want to coil, twine, knot, weave, or crochet, and how a particular fiber will develop in the selected technique.

The variety of available fibers is vast and a listing here would be endless. Each material—cotton, linen, rayon, jute, sisal, and wool, is spun into so many varieties that one must constantly haunt stores and craft counters that carry the fibers. Specialized suppliers that cater to craftsmen, listed in the back of the book, may be contacted for sample cards.

Because of the variety of available materials, basketry affords a means for educating yourself gradually about fibers over a period of time. After you discover a set of fibers you like to work with, by all means exploit them to the fullest, but constantly seek and experiment with others and with combinations. The majority of fibers are created from animal, vegetable, and synthetic sources. They are usually sold by weight and are available in two-ounce, four-ounce and heavier skeins, cones, or hanks. Heavy ropes may be sold by the length.

Animal Fibers

These are threads, yarns, and cords of varying sizes and plies woven from the fur and hair of animals: wool from sheep, alpaca from llamas, mohair from goats, camels' hair from camels, horsehair from horses. Fleece refers to the coat of wool that covers a sheep or other animal. When fleece is carded and pulled into lengths, preparatory to spinning, it is called "roving." Roving is soft and fluffy and often is used as the core in coiled basketry. When spun strands are twisted together, each strand is a "ply." Hence you will find thread and ropes labeled 2-ply, 6-ply, and so forth.

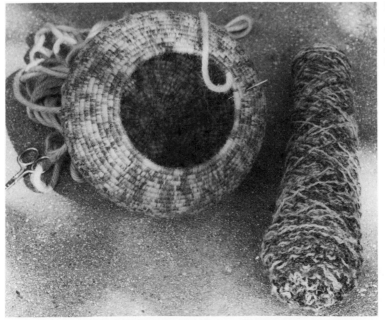

BASKET IN PROGRESS. Kathy Malec. Variegated yarns (also called space-dyed) result in two or more colorations within one cone of yarn. When used in basketry, a random coloring results.

Vegetable Fibers

Fibers spun from plants are considered vegetable fibers: cotton from the cotton shrub, linen from the flax plant, jute from the jute plant, and hemp from the hemp plant. Cotton and linen are fine fibers compared to jute and sisal, which are made into both coarse and fine fibers. Think of cotton sewing thread and cotton clothesline to visualize the difference in cotton fibers. Jute and sisal are readily available at hardware store counters in many diameters and strengths for every kind of job from tying small packages to hauling and mooring boats. Prickly cords such as jute and sisal should be lightly dampened with a sponge and water before handling, so they will be less scratchy.

Multiple-strand jute is a favorite of many craftsmen. Thin strands of jute are twisted into one thick strand. The strands may be separated to achieve thick and thin areas and negative spaces. One-hundred-strand jute measures about ¾ inch in diameter. You can combine strands yourself and work these the same way.

When searching for thick cords, ropes, and so forth, look in your classified pages for marine suppliers and cordage companies. In rural and urban communities, you will find large selections of cords at Ace Hardware stores, Sears Roebuck, and similar outlets.

Synthetic or Man-made Fibers

There is an incredible variety of synthetic fibers on the market. Since man learned to spin fibers from chemical compounds, an entire new industry developed. Rayon, one of the first synthetic fibers produced, was created as a substitute for silk produced by the silkworm. You will also discover such products as Nylon, Dynel, Orlon, Acrylic, and Orlon-Acrylic. There are blends of synthetic and animal and synthetic and vegetable yarns that may offer exactly the sheen, strength, and color you like. Fiber content affects coloring absorption so that a bright green rayon will have more sparkle than a bright green wool. The surface of a fiber must be considered when planning a basket. A slippery material, such as rayon, for example, is more difficult to coil than the rough fiber wools and jutes.

Other Fibers

Your constant foray into fibers for basketry will yield infinite types of yarns, ropes, and twines with exciting appearances, colors, textures, and strengths. These are called novelty yarns and are:

Plain: those with straight strands that are evenly twisted or braided.

Novelty: nubby varieties with bumps and thin and thick uneven surfaces.

Looped: those with thin and thick spirals and liny, tight twists that appear along a basic thread.

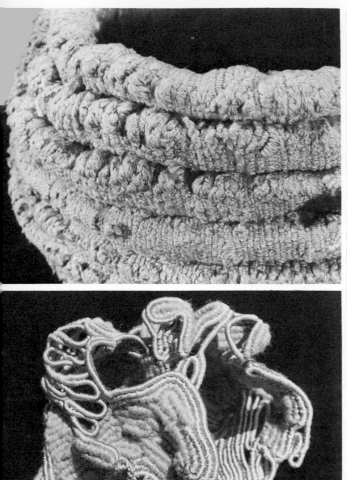

Above:
BASKETRY HANGING (detail). Jean Lamon. A jute core, wrapped with linen, has been painted with acrylic for a hard, lustrous finish.

Top, left:
WOVEN COILED BASKET (detail). Gary Trentham. Novelty yarns with thick and thin portions produce interesting textures in a woven tube that has been stuffed and coiled.

Above, left:
UNTITLED. Joan Austin. Combining dull fuzzy yarns with shiny slick silks and rayons results in a contemporary statement.

Bottom:
SEUSS POT. Gayle Luchessa. Stripped and shredded lengths of colored rags are worked into a free-form basket along with jutes and other cords that have been knotted.

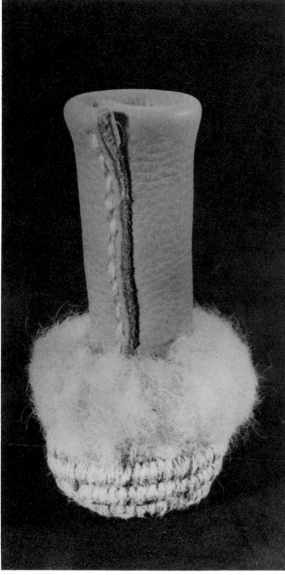

Above:
MINI-POT. Geoff Welch. 5 inches high, 3-inch diameter. Leather and lamb's wool have been combined with a wool-coiled pot form.

Top, right:
SCULPTURE BASKET. Lew Gilchrist. 11 inches high, 13-inch diameter. White wool yarn with pheasant and goose feathers. The coiled form is sculptural.

Bottom:
CARACUL CONTAINER. Marie Waters. 6½ inches high, 9-inch diameter. Handspun caracul wool over a jute core, colored with peach-leaf dye.

Courtesy, artist

You can dye yarns all one color or in multiple tones. To avoid tangling, always tie a loosely wound skein before placing it in the dye bath. For variegated coloring, use tie-dye methods explained below.

COLORS AND FIBERS

Fibers are available in natural and dyed shades. Whether you buy industrially colored yarns or dye your own fibers with vegetable or synthetic dyes, there is always a tendency for the colors to fade, in time, from sunlight and incandescent light. When fading is not a factor, use any colors you like. When fading will be detrimental to the finished objects you may prefer adhering to natural colors.

If a fiber will be used in conjunction with grasses that must be constantly moistened to keep them workable, the dyed fiber may fade or shrink. This is a real problem in modern basketry, and only time and experience will give you answers about the colorfastness of specific materials. Pre-test materials for the necessary exposure and durability factors you require before working them into a complete project.

For variegated color (also called "space dyeing" because the yarn is dyed at intervals) use tie-dye techniques. Tightly bind off portions of the skein with rubber bands where you do not want color. If you want two colors, you will have to tie off two sections, dye, then untie one section and redye. The overdyeing will change the first color. For multiple coloring bind off portions with dyed yarns of nonfast colors; the colors from the bindings will bleed onto the original cord when it is placed in the dyebath.

PLASTICS AND OTHER MATERIALS

Many of the baskets emphasize the artist's continuing ability to depart from tradition in his search for new and unusual materials. You won't get these materials from usual craft supply sources; they are improvised from industrially oriented products or from whatever is available. Try the plastic tubing used to aerate fish aquariums and for medical purposes. Use electric wire, telephone wire, and plastic fishing line. Rubber and elastic products can offer many surprises. A good wrapping material for

UNTITLED (detail). Bonnie Zimmer. Strips of screen wire have been rolled to use as the coil that is held together with doubled wires in an improvised twining technique. The center core is woven wire.

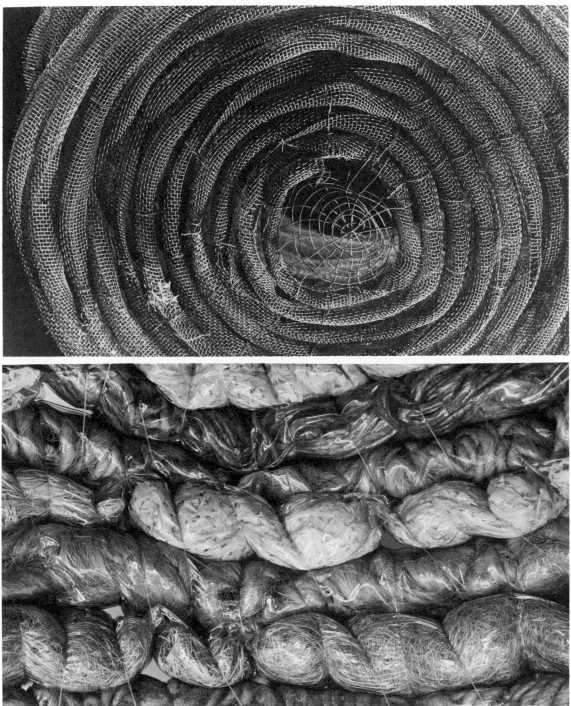

UNTITLED (detail). Gyongy Laky. Casing material used for cold cuts was stuffed with various fibers—sisal, straw, packing scraps, and so forth, then coiled and held together with plastic fishline.

Photographed at the Richmond Art
Center, Richmond, California

Left:
HANGING POT. Kathryn McCardle. 24 inches high, 12-inch diameter. Plastic tubing worked over a rope core using coiling and knotting. Added pieces of plastic are inserted between the coils and then knotted. Some of the tubes have beads within for color and design.

Top:
SPACE SIPHON. Budd Stalnaker. 3½ inches high, 7-inch diameter. Linen yarns clove-hitched over a coiled core of polyurethane. Brass ending on the siphon tube.

Courtesy, artist

Bottom:
COILED WIRE. Suellen Glashausser. Plastic electric wire is handled as the weft materials wrapped around flat plastic stripping.

Courtesy, artist

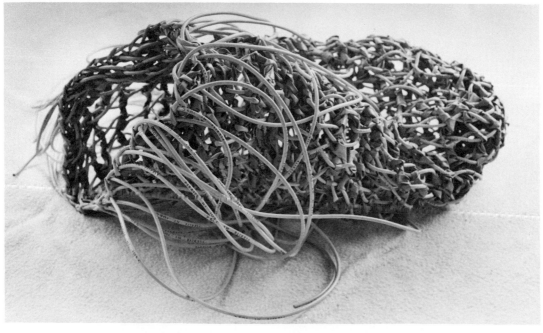

coiling can be made from plastic sandwich wrap and bread wrappers. Pull the width of plastic wrap through the hole in a spool of thread and twist it as you pull. The result is a strong strand of clear or printed plastic. Synthetic raffia, made from plastic compounds, is available in many colors wherever craft and hobby supplies are sold. Also experiment with materials used for trimming hats and available from millinery suppliers. Some of this comes in narrow, medium, and wide woven plastic and fiber combinations.

GRASSES

It is difficult to conjecture whether the primitive basketmaker would envy his modern counterpart when it came to gathering materials. The modern basketmaker can flip open to the page of a catalog and readily order many of the materials that his predecessors had to spend hours harvesting and preparing. The ease of securing materials has increased the popularity of basketmaking; yet many craftsmen do enjoy hunting for their materials, pulling them from the natural source, drying, and preparing them. For those who are involved in a back-to-the-earth philosophy, perhaps basketmaking is one of the most enjoyable ancient crafts to be revived.

With the revival of basketmaking, many suppliers have a ready stock of the materials pictured at right. Round reeds are available in standard sizes that relate to the diameter of the reed.

Size 1, diameter $\frac{1}{16}$ inch
Size 2, diameter $\frac{5}{64}$ inch
Size 3, diameter $\frac{3}{32}$ inch
Size 4, diameter $\frac{7}{64}$ inch
Size 5, diameter $\frac{1}{8}$ inch
Size 6, diameter $\frac{11}{64}$ inch

Flat reed is about $\frac{1}{2}$ inch wide.

Reed is sold in one-pound coils that average about six feet in length. Willow, ash, and caning can be purchased in the different widths and also in coils. Natural raffia, paper twine, coconut palm, sea grass, munj, and others are usually sold by weight. Because of the various weights and sizes of these materials, it is difficult to determine how long a piece you will get in a pound. If you are ordering by mail, through a catalog, your first order will almost always be experimental. You might ask for a few yards of each material which the company can cut from a coil, weigh, and charge for accordingly. When you receive your order, measure and weigh the material, see how far it will go in a given project, and interpolate your needs from a basic formula.

If you prefer to harvest your own materials, you will have to gain a knowledge of the materials in your area, what part of the plant can be used for the purpose, when each element is ripe, and the tools needed for gathering.

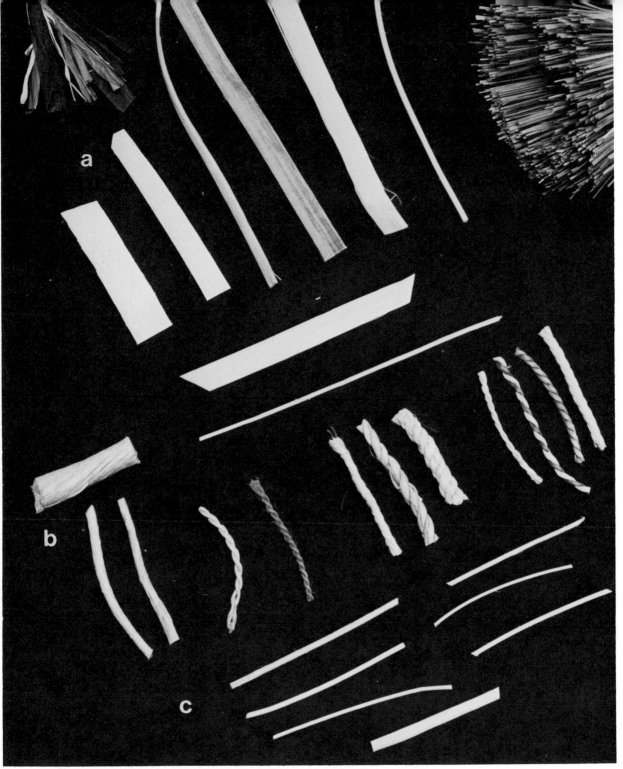

The above is a sampling of easily available traditional basketmaking materials:

Row a. (*left to right*) Natural raffia in natural and dyed colors, 1 inch and ⅝ inch flat ash splint, ⅜ inch and ¼ inch flat reed, ¼ inch round and flat reed, wood spline, corn husk, round willow.

Row b. (*left to right*) Paper twine (twisted) 3 thicknesses, palmetto, twisted coconut fiber, handspun munj (palm) yarn in 3 thicknesses, sea grass in different thicknesses and colors.

Row c. Round reed in a variety of sizes; cane, flat and round.

Samples, courtesy, The Yarn Loft,
Del Mar, California

Preparing fresh materials may require storing them away and drying, then learning to peel, split, make splints, twist, color, and so forth. With each material, annotate your results carefully, so you can repeat them in a subsequent harvest.

Woods and grasses usually are brittle and hard when dry. To make them supple soak them in warm water so they can be manipulated in coiling, weaving, knotting, and twining. Usually, the harder the outer skin and the closer the inner fibers, the longer the soaking time required. Thick brown willow may have to be soaked for a week, then stored in plastic bags to keep it damp until using. But none of the wood or grass should be stored damp for too long a time, or it will tend to mildew and form mold, which can be detrimental to the finished form.

In different geographic areas, materials common to the vicinity may be purchased or harvested for basketry. In tropical and subtropical climates, coconut-palm fronds are abundant and show up in the native baskets. Coconut-palm-leaf baskets are woven by peoples of Oceania. Panama hats are woven from carefully selected, oiled, and sun-dried leaves of a *Carludovica palmata* native to Ecuador, Colombia, Central America, and Jamaica. Brownish baskets from Malaysia reflect the abundance of the rattan that grows in the area.

Peoples in temperate zones tend to use an indigenous variety of plants such as reeds, rushes, and sedges that flourish in marsh areas in many parts of the world. A study of American Indian baskets and the materials used gives archaeologists insight as to the vegetation of particular areas at certain times in history. Conversely, a basket of unknown origin can frequently be traced to a region by its material as well as by its design and form.

With the exception of the readily available grasses offered commercially, the craftsman who wishes to work with materials he has harvested will have to learn by trial and error or from older craftsmen who have an empirical knowledge of the area and its materials. Some information about preparing specific roots and grasses can be found in books dealing with Indian basketry and Indian crafts, such as *Indian Basketry* by George Wharton James; *Aboriginal Indian Basketry* by Otis T. Mason; and *Pomo Basketmaking* by Elsie Allen. Other good reference volumes are *Coconut Palm Frond Weaving* by William H. Goodloe and *Spruce Root Basketry of the Alaska Tlingit* by Frances Paul.

Pine needles, corn husks, kelp, raffia, bulrushes, cane, bamboo, straw, willow, cattail plants, and California redbud are among the materials used in the baskets illustrated throughout the various chapters. Most often, these are used in conjunction with fibers; in a few examples, entire baskets have been made from the natural grass, and these were selected not so much for the material used as for the contemporary form and artistic quality of the piece.

Coloring Natural Materials

Many natural materials can be dyed successfully, and one can again take a cue from baskets made by American Indians. Baskets that are

Bamboo is extremely versatile: its sticks can be used for spokes; it can be split into very fine strips for weaving.

Buckhorn plantain is one of many grasses that can be harvested when dry and its leaves and stems split and moistened for weaving.

Palm fronds are a favored basketry material of many cultures. The fronds can be used wide or split into fine strands.

Cane, raffia, wood strips, and other grasses are worked when damp. They may be soaked for several hours, depending upon the materials, then kept damp in a plastic bag. Use fast dye colors so they won't run when the work is dampened, and so the completed basket will not fade from daylight and sunlight.

scores of years old were colored with vegetable materials such as onion skins, cochineal, and whatever was available. The same materials can be used today, and any of the excellent books on dyeing with natural dyes, listed in the Bibliography, will suggest necessary formulae. One can also use the commercially prepared dyes such as Rit, Fibrec, Cushings, Putnam, and others. Each has different properties, so experiment until you achieve the results you want. Instant coffee can stain wood such as ash and oak. Use any prepared wood stain, paints, and varnishes that can be sprayed or brushed.

Cattail leaves, rushes, corn husks, and raffia that dry naturally require resoaking before putting into the dyebath. These materials usually are brittle when they are dried, but resoaking restores their moisture and makes them strong. They will probably require resoaking again before using and they should be worked while moist.

You can also dye a finished form by dipping the entire piece into

Indian Baskets. Hand-split ash twined and woven with sweet grass.

Collection, Audrey Sylvester
Durham, New Hampshire

dye. Designs can be added by handpainting or by masking off some areas and then painting with spray or brush. Felt-tip markers can be used, too.

It is important to reemphasize that hard, dry grasses and woods require moistening to be worked. If you are developing a basket with moistened materials and you have to set it aside, you can place the entire form in a pail of water until you are ready to come back to it. A plastic bag will hold in moisture for awhile, also, but never store a moistened piece too long or mildew will develop.

Hard materials cannot be coiled with a needle, as can fibers. Therefore, when coiling, sharpen the end of the weft material with a scissors or sharp knife to make it needlelike; work with the sharpened point as though it were a needle. When weaving or coiling becomes difficult, use an awl to open up the weave and to make room for the new piece and pull the piece through with a pliers, when necessary. If the materials tend to leave slivers, wear gloves.

BASKET. Lucy Traber. 11-inch diameter. Stripped cattail is twined over warp made of sedge roots, which are tough and woody. They must be soaked so they can be shaped.

Courtesy, artist

<

BROOMSTRAW BASKET. Molly Baross. 18 inches high, 7-inch diameter at base. Twining. Colored raffia is twined over broomstraw.

BASKET. Molly Baross. 5 inches high, 7 inches wide, 6 inches deep. Palm fronds are woven and twined.

Opposite page, top:
WOVEN AND TWINED PALM LEAVES. Lucy Traber. 34-inch diameter. Observe how plain weaving, used for the base, is combined with twining for the sides. The warp ends are flattened and allowed to protrude for an unusual solution to finishing a basket.
Courtesy, artist

Opposite page, bottom:
BASKET. Lucy Traber. 12-inch diameter. Twined kelp. Kelp is a fleshy seaweed found in the Pacific Ocean; Ms. Traber has harvested, prepared, and worked it into a basket.

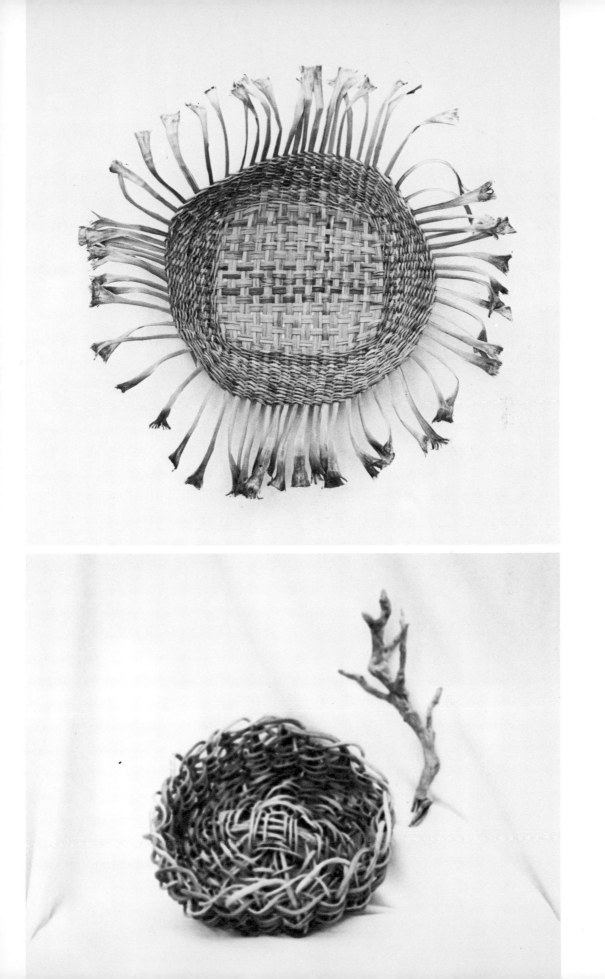

Basket. Contemporary Indian. Sweet grass woven and twined over brown ash warp. The form is a straightforward utilitarian container. The materials and colors could be emulated, but the contemporary craftsman is likely to be more inventive and innovative in the shapes he creates.

Collection, Audrey Sylvester
Durham, New Hampshire
Photo, Jack Adams

3

Sources and Ideas for
Basketry Forms and Designs

The beauty of an emerging new art form is that there are no set precedents and few conceived notions about form, textures, color combinations, and other elements of design. Historical examples of baskets can, of course, be used to stimulate ideas, shapes, and surface decorations. We can study a Pomo Indian basket and admire the craftsmanship, the swing of the form, the application of feathers and beads. But there would be no point in trying to copy a Pomo basket exactly. The object is to translate the visual impression a Pomo basket makes on your creative senses and, by borrowing the technique and embellishments, to invent a modern statement.

Many traditional basket shapes can be beautifully translated into new statements with fibers or with fibers and grasses. The Indian burden basket on page 106 has its modern counterparts in the examples on pages 107 and 209. A fishing basket of an Oceania tribe inspired Kathryn McCardle's sparsely twined basket on page 173. The examples illustrated in Chapter 1 can be used as a springboard for forms that you can develop in today's materials.

The artist who studies baskets of tribal cultures may not think of them as utilitarian containers. He observes their sculptural qualities: the size of the negative areas in relation to the woven areas, and the kinds of weaves used. He may see a purely decorative motif or a mechanical aspect in the finish of an edge that he can apply to a form that is completely different from the one he is studying. He uses bits and pieces from a multitude of visual and mental images. He wrestles with a different set of structural and functional problems than did his ancestors.

The artist is also stimulated by sources other than baskets. The examples in this chapter have been selected specifically to emphasize this search for form in organic and man-made shapes unrelated to baskets. You will find them in fruits, vegetables, and other plants and in ancient and modern ceramic and bronze vessels. These are offered in the hope that they will stimulate you and set you on your own course of observations. Study Greek, Indian, and Chinese pots, illustrated manscripts, and English heraldry designs for both shape and surface patterns.

Texture, an import element of basketry, can be achieved by thinking in terms of combining yarns with opposite qualities: soft with hard, shiny with dull, smooth with rough. Work with plied yarns and unply portions of them. Use grasses with fibers. Brush the yarns with a wire brush to bring out a texture and to make the wool more nubby.

Study color combinations in nature's objects and emulate these combinations in your baskets. Take color schemes from commercial fabrics or from master paintings, or work with the natural tones of the materials.

Good design is a matter of opinion and sensitivity. When you strive to incorporate the elements of design applied to all art forms, the result will be worth the study and effort involved.

A snail has the appearance of a coiled basket and could inspire colors, shaping, and band patterns.

FALL. Molly Baross. 6 inches high, 9 inches wide. Willow reed warp with colored raffia twined as the weft. Raffia was colored with commercial dyes in two colors and then both colors worked simultaneously in the twining method so that variations in color would occur and the basket would have the effect of Indian summer corn. The shape might have been inspired by the bill of a toucan (*below*).

A toucan's bill, or those of other birds, should be explored for shaping basket forms. The natural coloring of the bird could also suggest color combinations—in this case, black and yellow, with a touch of orange.

UNTITLED. Linda Ann Valeri. 3 inches high, 8 inches wide, 6 inches deep. Twined natural reed and raffia with pheasant feathers. Some black-dyed raffia around neck. The shape could have been patterned after a tuberous herb such as a canna or dahlia.

BIRD FORM. Joan Austin. Rattan warp is joined and shaped by twining with fibers. Birds are excellent forms for basket and sculptural shapes using basketry techniques.

GREEN CANE. Molly Baross. 10 inches high, 10 inches wide, 7 inches deep. Dyed cane was twined over dyed cane spokes. The top edge was finished with dyed raffia. Ms. Baross's experiment attempted to make the stiff fibers assume a soft appearance. The cane material was very hard to manipulate and the basket had to be continually soaked in hot water as the work progressed.

The huge tomato could easily have been the inspiration for the basket above. It wasn't, but such organic forms should be studied for potential basket shapes and for beginning and finishing ideas.

UNTITLED. Bonnie Zimmer. 10 inches high, 10-inch diameter. Clove hitching with various color linens.
Courtesy, artist

STAR BASKET. Kathy Malec. 6½ inches high, 9-inch diameter. Exposed core coiling. Mohair and wool.
Collection, Ronald Grace, Chicago

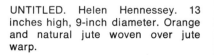

UNTITLED. Helen Hennessey. 13 inches high, 9-inch diameter. Orange and natural jute woven over jute warp.

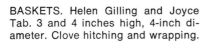

BASKETS. Helen Gilling and Joyce Tab. 3 and 4 inches high, 4-inch diameter. Clove hitching and wrapping.

UNTITLED. Joan Sterrenburg. 15 inches high. Gray polytwine and orange and black raffia twined over sisal.

Collection, W. R. Griffith,
Bloomington, Indiana
Courtesy, artist

COILED NECKLACES. Helen Hennessey. Wool and novelty yarns coiled over jute. Feathers added.

UNTITLED. Joan Sterrenburg. 25 inches high, 15-inch diameter. Crocheted polytwine with a cardwoven silk band to bind tip and secure peacock feathers.
Collection, D. W. Griffith, Bloomington, Indiana
Courtesy, artist

RED AND BLACK. Gary Trentham. 12 inches high, 15-inch diameter. Clove-hitched red wool with overhand knot endings. French knots added with black thread.

UNTITLED. Julie Connell. Twined and woven wool over cane and wood.

Courtesy, artist

RED OWL. Louise Robbins. 7 inches high, 7-inch diameter. Rings are 12 inches wide. Coiling. Wool and linen with guinea hen feathers.

COFFEE POT. Renie Adams. 15 inches high, 6-inch diameter. 10 inches wide handle to spout top. Variegated blue and white cotton crocheted and lightly stuffed.

SPRING. Molly Baross. 14 inches high, 7-inch diameter. Dyed raffia twined over cane warp.

BASKET. Pat Malarchar. 6 inches high. Twining. Jute warp and weft.

Courtesy, artist

CAT CONTAINER. Mary Lou Higgins. Crocheted acrilan, beads, lynx fur.
Photo, Ed Higgins

STANDING CYLINDER. Suellen Glashausser. Clove hitching with lawn chair webbing.
Courtesy, artist

UNTITLED. Ferne Jacobs. 7 inches high. Coiling. Mixed yarns.
Courtesy, artist

PEDESTAL BASKET I. Richard Daehnert. 25 inches high, 16-inch diameter. Coiling. Wool over jute with feathers. Three separate pieces assembled.
Courtesy, artist

SEED POD. Helen Hennessey. Coiling is accomplished with the Figure Eight stitch; coils are sewn together. The center core is removable. Novelty yarns and beads simulate the pistil and stamen.

A real flower such as this certainly could have inspired Helen Hennessey's piece, above.

>

MOUNTAIN. Ferne Jacobs. 10 inches high, 10-inch diameter. Dull raffia and shiny metallic threads with multicolored yarns coiled with the Lazy Squaw stitch recreate a quiet mountain shape.

Courtesy, artist

Stana Coleman's basket form is shaped remarkably like the onion, below, photographed at an outdoor market in Italy. The basket is twined and wrapped. 11 inches high, 5-inch diameter.

Three coiled forms by Pat Williams reflect an interest in seashells. The top coiled basket (rear view shown) is shaped like a giant conch shell. It incorporates a removable inner form that is similar to the animal within the shell. 3½ inches high, 6½ inches wide, 4 inches deep. The shape (*right*) could have been inspired by a bone, shell, or piece of coral. It is 2½ inches high, 5 inches wide, 4 inches deep. A tiny basket only 1 inch high and 1½ inches in diameter helps to illustrate the versatility of the traditional coiling technique for free-form large and small shapes. All pieces are made of linen over a jute core using the Figure Eight and Lazy Squaw stitches.

Bones have fascinating indentations, protrusions, and negative spaces that can be used to simulate forms made with basketry techniques.

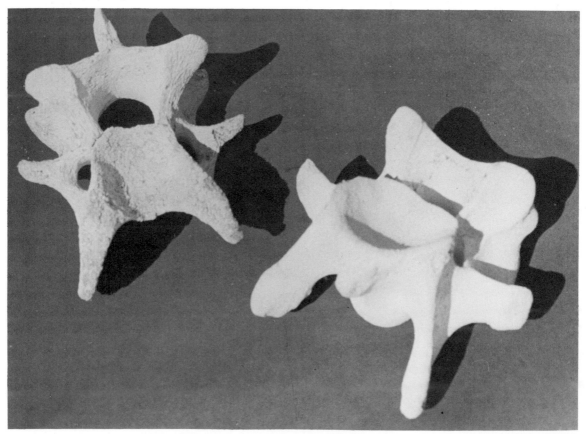

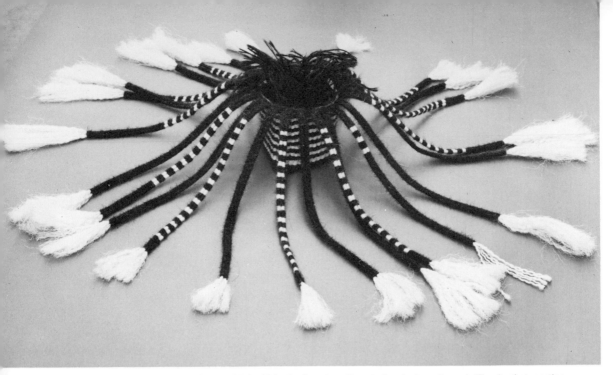

BASKET FORM. Budd Stalnaker. 13 inches high, 60-inch diameter. Horsehair, sisal, and wool. The basket portion is twined, the extensions are Figure Eight wrapped. Added black strands protrude from inside the basket.
Courtesy, artist

FREE-FORM BASKET. Joan Austin. Textured novelty yarns and sisal. Shells help emphasize the organic appearance of the entire piece. Adding shells onto warp ends remaining on a twined basket is an excellent solution for finishing in an attractive manner.

THREE-LEGGED BASKET. Gladamay Henrikson. 10 inches high, 6-inch diameter. Reed, raffia, and wood beads. Coiling and twining. A three-legged bronze pot from the ancient Chinese Shang dynasty inspired this contemporary basketry statement.

Courtesy, artist

Bottom, left:
A bronze Yu from the early Chou period, China (about 1000 B.C.) can suggest overall basket shapes, handle attachment devices, patterns, and motifs for a modern basketmaker.

Private Collection

Bottom, right:
A design, such as this, worked into the base of a bronze Chou pot, is similar to many patterns in the baskets of American Indians.

Double Jar. Pottery, Amlash area, Persia, 9th to 8th century B.C. Can be studied for its simplicity of form and the animallike head. Combining two or more basket shapes could result in a modern fiber statement.

Private Collection

Bottom, left:
DOTS AND DONUTS. David F. Silverman. A modern ceramic form could also be used to inspire basket shapes.

Bottom, right:
Spouted Ewer. Iran 1000 to 700 B.C. It is also simply shaped, with handles and animal symbol added. Natural history and art museums are rich in design sources for basketry.

Private Collection

A Yam Mask corroborates the ability to achieve unusual shapes with the coiling techniques. Such masks
should be studied for added motifs, how portions are
assembled, and how elements are added and the
edges finished.

Private Collection

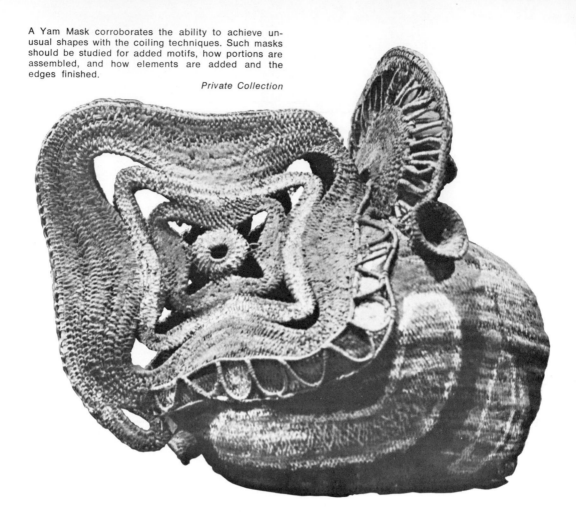

A plain woven basket can be decorated by stenciling
and painting. The same basket has been carefully
masked so that the top and bottom have two different
designs.

*Linda Cross for Illinois Bronze
Paint Company, Lake Zurich, Illinois*

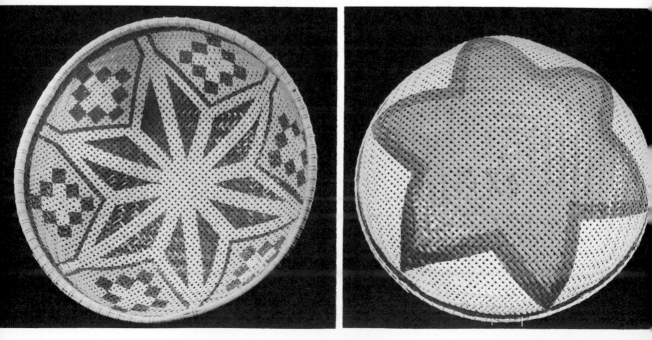

Basket Display. Wolfram Krank. Various baskets emulate Indian designs with a touch of modern creative artistry. All are coiled using the Figure Eight and Lazy Squaw stitches.

Courtesy, artist

INSIDE OF MOUNTAIN. Ferne Jacobs. 10 inches high, 10-inch diameter. Raffia, metallic threads, and multicolored yarns. Inside view of "Mountain," page 57, shows the structure and form that are as carefully designed as the exterior. Figure Eight and Lazy Squaw coiling.

4

Coiling

The coiling method for making baskets has been employed for centuries in almost every culture, but it is a relatively new skill for the majority of modern craftsmen who have been accustomed to weaving, macramé, crochet, and knitting. Those who have discovered the versatility of the technique are excited about the variety it offers not only for making baskets but also for sculptural forms that can employ basketry and other techniques. Coiling becomes another tool in the expanding workbasket of the modern artist-craftsman.

There are different definitions of coiling. One authority refers to it as "a sewing technique [that] consists of sewing a spiral foundation of twigs, grass, or other material securely in a coil and wrapping this coil with another material that is threaded through a needle and sewn over the coils." Another resource describes coil-binding as "a weaving technique; a firm but flexible material is used for the wrap, or coil. The weft material should be fine so it can be threaded through a needle." Both are right and wrong in the contemporary context.

For clarity, and to conform to modern terminology, the concept of weaving will be used:
"Core" or "coil" will indicate the warp, and for coiling the words "core" and "coil" will be used.
The "weft" will be the wrapping material; this is the thread that binds the core together in a coil.

Two basic stitches are used for working the weft around the core: the Lazy Squaw and the Figure Eight. These are clearly demonstrated, followed by variations and additional stitches. Various basketry books call some of the related stitches by different names. The Lace Stitch is the same as the Mariposa Knot weave or Samoan Lace weave. Klikitat and imbrication are the same. And the Buttonhole Stitch used in basketry is the same as that used in embroidery. Several wrapping methods are explained,

65

and these are borrowed from macramé and weaving techniques. Do not be hampered by thinking you must use only the pure forms seen on traditional baskets; combine any technique you know so long as it works. If you have to join two pieces of yarn together, do it by any method you can —sewing, knotting, overlapping, or gluing.

A coiled basket is usually begun from a center bottom, and several ways of beginning a bottom are illustrated. It is suggested that you make a sampler so you learn all the variations on one piece at one time. With this knowledge at your fingertips you can decide how to proceed to create any basket shape and how to incorporate in surface decorations and added elements.

Coiling is not the fastest method of building up a form, so, for a first project, plan a small piece or use relatively heavy yarns so you can get the feel of the technique and the shaping potential. Think in terms of

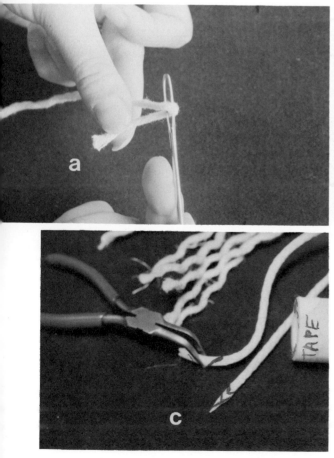

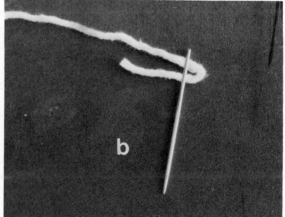

When soft yarns defy needle-threading, a good technique is to (a) crease the yarn over the head of the needle, then (b) thread the folded portion through the needle. Threads or ropes that will not fit through a needle may be pulled through with an awl. They can be placed through a hairpin or piece of stiff wire shaped with an eye ending. (c) You can make the end of a heavy rope very stiff and needlelike by wrapping it tightly with a piece of adhesive tape, and, if necessary, pulling the rope through the coils with a pliers. In some situations you can tape the end of a thick yarn to a needle eye if the yarn will not fit the eye.

assembling two or more parts as illustrated in the examples beginning on page 110.

Finishing the ends and tops of the baskets neatly and attractively is always a problem regardless of the technique used. The examples will suggest many solutions. You can buttonhole-stitch, whipstitch, wrap a new color cord and sew it to the original, stitch a strip of fabric over an edge, and so forth. Be innovative in finishing methods and seek contemporary materials to solve any problems. For example: When you want added cords to be stiff and to protrude in tortured ways, wrap a piece of wire into the cord; or set the fiber in the shape you want, secure it with hair clips, and spray or dip it in starch, hair spray, a clear nail polish, or glue.

In addition to the baskets that illustrate the various stitches and working methods, there are sections showing basketry applied to masks, sculpture, and jewelry, and a gallery of basketry ideas.

THE SAMPLER

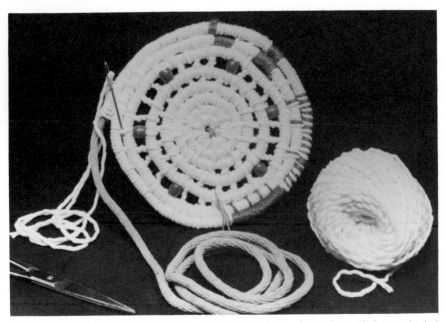

It is a practical idea to make a coiled "sampler" to learn the various stitches and what they do. Once you know the basic techniques you realize how simple it is to shape and to add color and decorative items. For this sampler, a core of cotton clothesline was used with white cotton cable cord and colored Jute-tone. Use any thick, smooth cords that are available and that are not slippery or slick. You can study how the stitches work more easily with thick, smooth cords than with thin threads or with soft, fuzzy, and textured yarns.

BEGINNING THE COIL

1.   Trim the end of the core so it tapers. Thread a needle with a three-foot length of weft. Use the loose weft end and begin to wind the weft around the core about two inches from the end, overlapping the first wind to hold it firm. Wind to about ½ inch from tapered end of core.

2.   Bend the core and pull the weft through the center of the core with the needle end. Catch the tapered end and begin to make a loop. Always wrap very tightly.

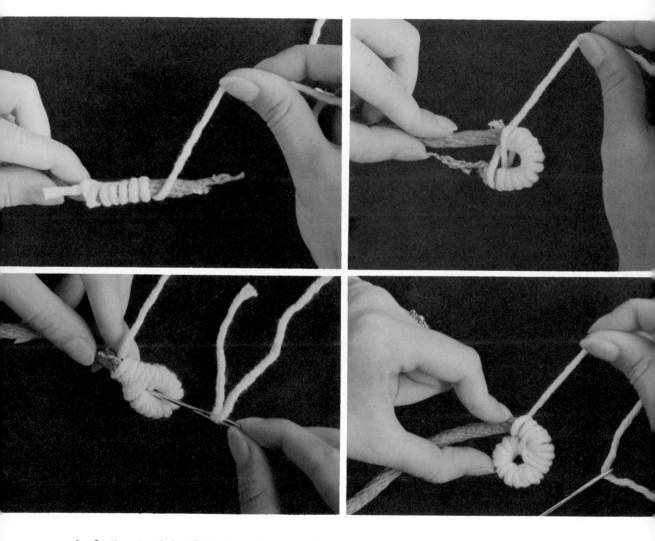

3.   Continue to wind until the tapered core end is secured to the solid core. Push the needle through the center of the loop.

4.   Bend the core to form a coil and bring the weft between the core, winding from front to back of the core. You are now ready to begin the Lazy Squaw stitch.

THE LAZY SQUAW STITCH

5. Wind the weft around the core four times from front to back. Then bring the weft from behind and over the core and into the center of the coil. Pull tightly and hold. Continue to wind four times around the core and bring the stitch into the center until you complete two coils. The Lazy Squaw is a visible stitch that spans two or more coils.

6. For the first two coils, the stitch will span both rows. Attach an identifying thread to the point where the coil has begun. Use this thread as your guide for the beginning of each new row, or your "point of movement." That way, your coil will always be round. If you change stitches or shaping at arbitrary places, the coil will tend to be crooked.

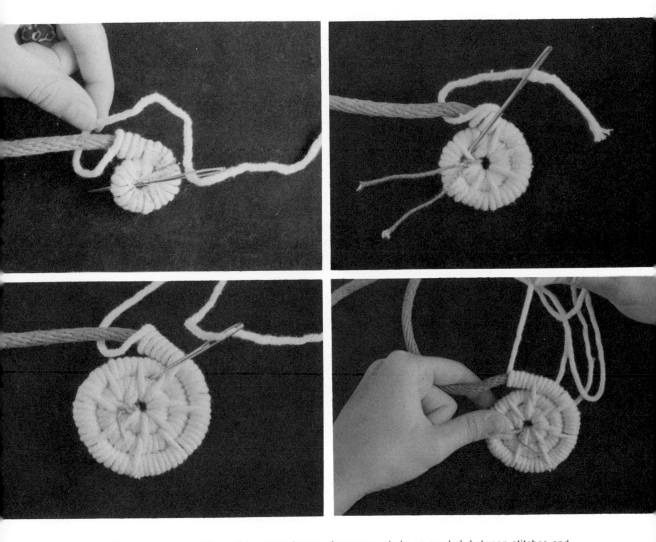

7. As the coiling progresses and the coil becomes larger, place more winds, as needed, between stitches and insert the needle over and between the coil below it. (Do *not* continually bring the stitch back to the center.) Form the habit of inserting the needle in from the front rather than the back of the work to simplify the procedure. You can see exactly where you are placing the needle when you want to create a pattern with the Lazy Squaw stitch. If you work so the needle is inserted from the back you will constantly have to turn the work over to find the pattern.

8. Always pull the warp very tight. Hold the coil in the left hand with the core coming from the left, and wind the weft with the right hand so it does not continually tangle around the core. If you are left-handed reverse the procedure. If you find yourself constantly untangling weft from the core, you are not holding the threads conveniently. Coiling is slow work, at best, and everything you can do to facilitate the procedure will yield a more enjoyable technique and a better result.

MUPPET (detail). Kathy Malec. Patterning made with the Lazy Squaw stitch is evident in this basket of white wool and rayon warp over a linen core. When two colors are used, one color must overlap the adjacent color. The Lazy Squaw stitches are carefully placed so they form a pattern. Where the coils expand in diameter, the apparent Lazy Squaw stitches are not close enough together to form both design and solidity; therefore the Figure Eight stitch (see following pages), which does not show, is interspersed.

>

The Lazy Squaw stitch produces a radiating pattern when carefully placed on the coil. With these examples, you should have no difficulty recognizing the stitch in any basket you pick up to study.

Examples of the Lazy Squaw stitch used with a broad weft are placed next to one another as the coil increases in size. You can shape a coil in any way you like—circular, rectangular, square, oval, and so forth, simply by how you form the beginning. In squares and rectangles the beginning can be at an end rather than in the center.

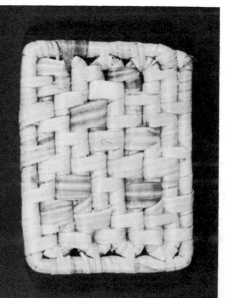

THE FIGURE EIGHT STITCH

1.   The Figure Eight stitch does not overlap two coils as does the Lazy Squaw; rather, it is worked between the coils and does not show. Wrap the weft around the core and, from the back, place your needle below the adjacent coil.

2.   Then bring the weft over coil (a) and behind coil (b). Wrap as many times as desired and repeat. This stitch is much stronger than the Lazy Squaw.

JUTE BASKET (detail). Gary Trentham. The Figure Eight worked with thick yarns does create an extra wind around each coil; but it does not span two coils as does the Lazy Squaw. When thin threads are used, the wrapping of one thread over another does not stand out. In this basket, it forms an additional texture because of the thickness of the jute weft. The fringe results from cords added between the coils after the basket is completed (see pages 108–109).

>

SEUSS POT. Gayle Luchessa. Jute, English mohair, and feathers. A combination of the Lazy Squaw and Figure Eight stitches. The Lazy Squaw is definitely used as a decorative element. Feathers are wrapped into the weft as the work progresses (see page 78).

LACE STITCH

1.   To create a space between the coils, and a lacy appearance, place a knot on the Lazy Squaw stitch before continuing to wrap. When the long strand of the Lazy Squaw stitch is over the coil, bring the weft over the strand from left to right; and behind it, as shown, and continue to wrap from back to front.

2.   For a greater separation between coils, make a double knot on the Lazy Squaw strand by wrapping with the weft two times. You can also cross over a Figure Eight stitch for another detail. Always pull the knot tight and hold the wefts tightly as you continue to wrap following a knot.

ADDING BEADS

3.   If you want a bead to sit *between* the coils rather than hang outside the basket, place it on a Figure Eight stitch. String the bead onto the weft as you bring the weft to the front of the coils. Insert the needle under the adjacent coil.

4.   Bring the needle behind the bottom coil, back through the bead from the bottom up, and then continue to wrap. A bead can be placed among lace stitches. If beads are stitched to the basket after it is finished, or placed on the wefts alone, they will protrude from the basket.

LACE STITCH BASKET SCULPTURE.
Eileen Bernard. 16 inches high, 6-inch
diameter. The double knot has been
used throughout the basket as a joining and a decorative element.
Photo, Lee Snadow

ADDING WEFT AND SPLICING CORE

1. As you progress with the sampler, you will have to add weft frequently. When there's about a two-inch end on the weft, thread a new weft and place the new end along the core. Wrap the end in with about one inch of the original weft.

2. Then lay the remaining inch of the original weft along the core and wrap it in with the new weft. Wrap very tightly so there is no evident bump from the addition.

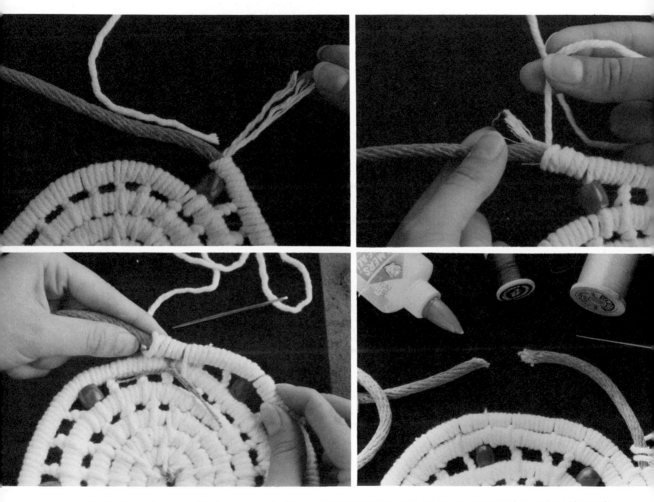

3. Continue to wrap with the new weft. As you change patterns and motifs on the sampler, and as the coils enlarge, tie another piece of "movement" cord onto a coil directly in line with the original point of movement cord at the center of the coil. Also add new lengths of weft by knotting two cords together and letting the knots become part of the motif at regular or irregular intervals. Use imagination and be inventive; there are no set rules.

TO SPLICE A CORE

4. Taper the ends then glue and/or stitch together. Be sure to wrap this joint very carefully and do not put too much tension on it. Different types of core materials will require different treatments. Cotton or wool roving can be spliced by tw.sting ends together. Cane, willow, and so forth, can be spliced by cutting ends different lengths and placing them on top of one another before proceeding with the wrapping.

ADDING COLORS

1. Continuing with your sampler, learn to add colors by several techniques so you'll know what they are when you need to use them. You may develop other methods that are equally as effective. A new color can be added the same way you splice in a new weft shown on the previous page. Place the new color weft on the core.

2. Adhere it to the core by wrapping a few winds with the original color, then wrap the original weft with the new color. (You are not necessarily using short ends.) You can carry a color along by wrapping it beneath the weft until you need it again. Or you can drop it behind the work and have it ready to use on the next row. You can add any number of colors; it's a very flexible, versatile method.

3. Remember, when you wrap in a new color and bind it to the adjacent coil, that color will show regardless of whether it is a Lazy Squaw or a Figure Eight stitch as it crosses the coil. When it shows, it should be developed as a decorative element.

4. If you do not want the second color to cross coils, wrap in a short section, then carry the color beneath the original weft and pick it up to use again as desired. As you work with this on the sampler, you'll understand the procedure.

1.   You can also wrap with two colors and two differently textured cords simultaneously. Both cords should be threaded through your needle and used for binding to the adjacent coil; here the binding is accomplished with a Figure Eight stitch. When a fine weft is used, it usually lies flat against the adjacent coil. The heavier the cord, the more it will show.

2.   Another way to add color while you are coiling is to work strands of new threads under the wrapping. These strands may be knotted or unraveled, or beads and feathers may be placed on them, and so forth. Color and other additional elements can be sewn between the coils and around stitches when the basket is completed. Observe the various techniques for adding elements beginning on page 106 and in the examples throughout the book.

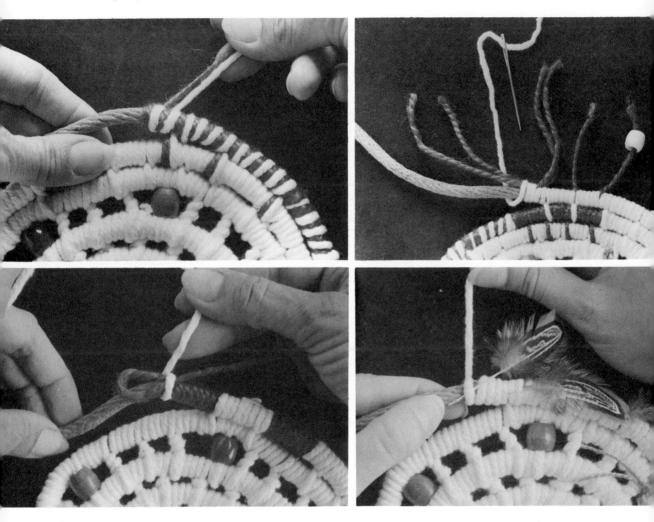

3.   If you want to continue a color from one coil to the next (see sampler) in a pattern, work in a color bar of X number of winds on the coil carrying the original color under the weft. Then fold the color thread, as shown, and bundle it up to keep it out of the way until you need it for the next coil. On the second coil you can increase or decrease the number of winds, depending upon the design desired.

ADDING FEATHERS

4.   Feathers are used extensively as a decorative element in basketry. It is best to strip the shaft of the feather by scraping it with a knife or scissors blade, then secure the shaft under the weft with about four winds and a Figure Eight stitch. Always place the quill in the opposite direction from the way you are wrapping so it doesn't get mangled and crushed in the wrapping procedure. Feathers may be sewn onto a basket after it is finished. Often they are wrapped onto hanging ends, as you will note in many examples.

FINISHING THE END OF THE COIL

Plan to bind off the end of the coil directly over the point of movement so the coil will not appear crooked. Taper the core end (*above*) and place an extra needle in with the wrap. Wind the weft around both the core and the needle and continue with whatever stitch you are using. Wind very tightly. Remove the extra needle (*below*) and replace it with the threaded needle and pull through all the winds, using a pliers if necessary. If the tip threads tend to slip, add a dab of glue or stitch them to the core with clear or a matching color thread.

Core ends can be used decoratively. Try adding extra threads to a core; unravel the core or add beads or feathers to it; it can be shaped as a handle or hanging device (see top photo, page 89).

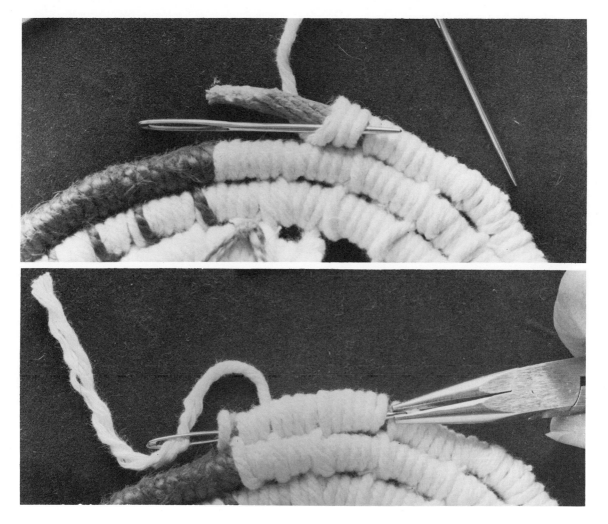

SHAPING

As you work the sampler, you can explore the idea of shaping. Or, begin a basket with the techniques you have learned and start to shape it. Shaping involves pulling the core tightly and placing it in the position you want the shape to take. You might want to work over a bowl, a ball, or a vase until you are able to shape by the eye and hand. Once you try it, you'll discover that it is simple and has no mystery to it whatsoever. Basic basket shapes are based on geometric solids: cube, cone, cylinder, and sphere, and all odd shapes are derived from these, regardless of the process used.

1. If you want to achieve a negative space in the wall of the basket, fold the core material back on itself until you build up a shape that outlines the hole.

2. You can also make a coil protrude beyond the circumference of a basket by pushing the core out to the shape desired and wrapping it without attaching it to an adjacent coil. A stiff core (such as sea grass, shown here) is best for protruding coils.

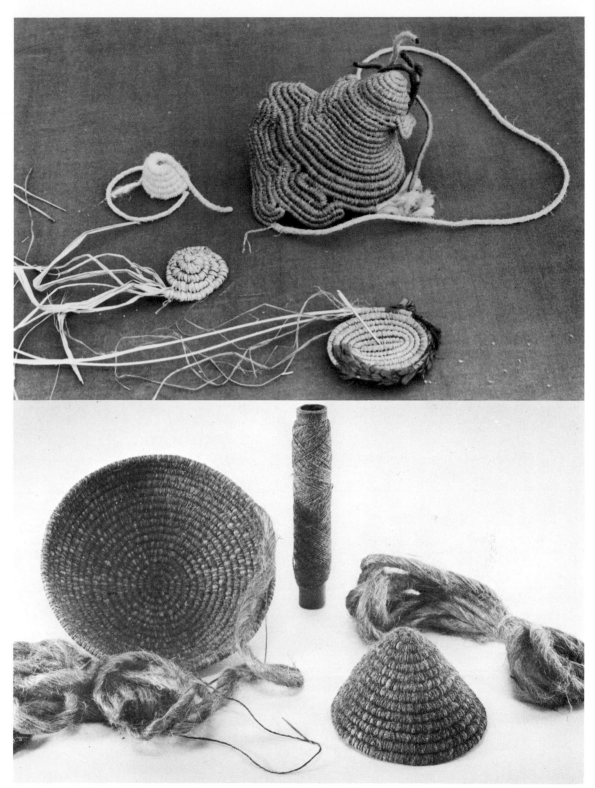

(*above*) An endless variety of shapes can be made with basketry techniques and materials whether the core is cane, willow, or rope. Coiling is extremely versatile for free form as well as traditional shapes. Soft, gray, unspun jute (*below*) assumes a rigidity and hardness when it is used as a core for horsehair and wool. The basket grows and takes shape as each coil's circumference is increased and placed on the preceding coil with the Figure Eight stitch. See following page for finished piece. Kathy Malec.

GRAY BASKET. Kathy Malec. 14 inches high, 9-inch diameter. Gray unspun jute with horsehair and wool wrapping. Colored wrapped strands are added to the top of the lid and the core material has been fluffed out. Notice that the wrapping is spaced so the unspun jute core shows in an exposed core technique.

>

BASKET. Mary Baughn. 5 inches high, 12-inch diameter. Coiling has been shaped in the traditional manner for the bottom of the basket; an open wiggly coil with wrapping has been used around the side. The edge is made separately as a series of coils folded back on one another, then stitched to the rim of the basket.

MUPPET. Kathy Malec. 5 inches high, 4-inch diameter. White wool, silk, and rayon over a linen core. Stone beads. Lazy Squaw and Figure Eight stitches. Observe how the color change occurs in the stitches and how they are used.

FREE FORM. Royce Zimon. 8½ inches high, 9 inches wide, 5 inches deep. Three shades of green wool over a spiral rubber telephone core result in wiggly, unusual shaping. Different shades of threads add to the design concept.

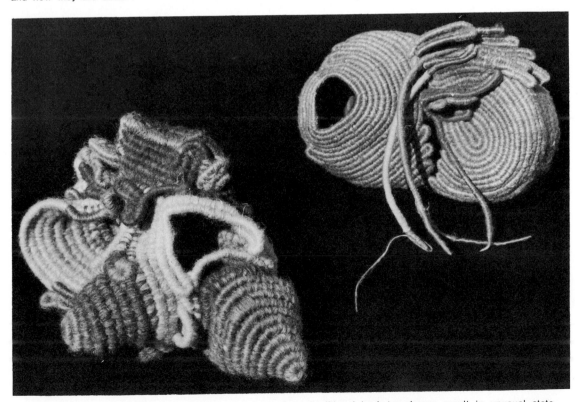

SCULPTURAL BASKETRY. Joan Austin. Departures from traditional basketry shapes result in unusual statements. Joan Austin masterfully combines colors, tight and loose coils, and different-textured yarns. She also combines two or more shapes by attaching them with a Figure Eight or Lazy Squaw stitch or by sewing them together where the joints do not show.

SEUSS BASKET. Gayle Luchessa. 15 inches high, 8 inches wide, 3 inches deep. English mohair with green and yellow linen over cotton roving core. Lazy Squaw and Figure Light stitching; multiple forms have been assembled in the removable lid. The color changes are carefully grouped and repeated in the borders of the lid forms.

MORE WRAPPING METHODS

Fibers wrapped around a coil using the Lazy Squaw and Figure Eight stitches are the foundation of traditional basketry techniques. Other wrapping methods frequently were used for holding bundled grasses together for handles. In contemporary basketry methods, fibers may be wrapped around one another for decorative endings, added elements, negative spaces, and other motifs. Several methods for wrapping fibers are illustrated to provide variety for different motifs and where structural problems must be solved.

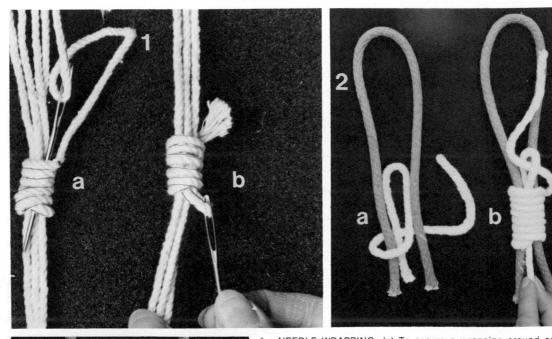

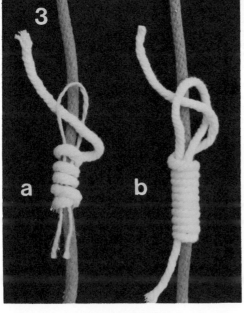

1. NEEDLE WRAPPING: (a) To secure a wrapping around one or more strands, overlap the first wind, then continue to wrap tightly, wrapping in an *unthreaded* needle. When the wrapping is completed, thread the needle and (b) pull it down through the wrapping. Snip off end of thread and twist the wrap to tighten.

2. TO WRAP TWO CORDS: A good method for wrapping handles and other projecting strands. (a) Fold the wrapping cord with a loop parallel to the cord to be wrapped. (b) Wind the wrapping cord and pull the end through the loop; pull the end down to secure the wrap.

3. CORD WRAPPING: Use this method when you do not have a needle or when the cord is too large to fit through the needle eye. It may be used for wrapping one or more strands. (a) Wrap an extra piece of doubled cord into the wrapping. When the desired length is wrapped, put the end of the wrapping cord through the loop and pull down into and through the wrap as in the needle wrap (*above*). (b) Self Cord Wrap: For wrapping a single thread, use a looped piece of the same wrapping cord laid parallel with the strand to be wrapped, as above. Put the end through the loop and pull down through the wrap.

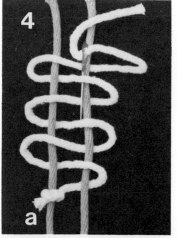

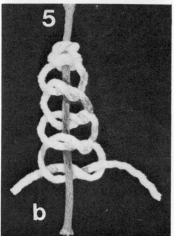

4. FIGURE EIGHT WRAP: A decorative wrapping for two cords or pairs of cords. The wrapping is executed in a Figure Eight around the two cords; the needle is placed along one cord and wrapped in, then threaded and pulled through the wrapping. (*Note:* when this is done the two cords will be tightly pulled together. They are separated here for demonstration purposes.)

5. THE OVERHAND KNOT WRAP. Another decorative motif can be worked over two or more cords by making an overhand knot first on the front of the cord, then bringing the two cords to the back and making another overhand knot. Repeat for as long as you like; secure ends into the wrapping with a crochet hook or needle.

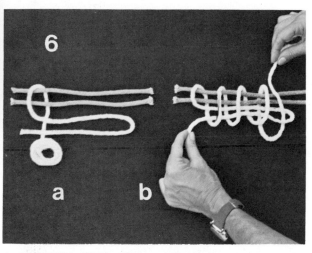

6. PERUVIAN WRAP. When multitude strands are to be wrapped and you want to introduce a new color try this wrap: (a) lay out the strands to be wrapped. Place the left end of the wrapping cord in a **U** shape parallel to strands; bring the right over, around, and under the strands and under the **U** shape, as shown. (b) Continue to wind until you are near the bottom of the **U**. (A loose wind is shown for demonstration purposes but the winds should be tight and close together.) On the last wind, bring the right end through the **U** and hold with a finger. Pull the left end up, release your finger, and the right end will travel up with the pull to tighten the wrap. Cut the ends close to the wrap and tuck under if necessary.

HANGING BASKET (detail). Doris Hoover. Wrapped coils are combined with wrapped circles and lengths of different-sized fibers. The wrapped shapes may be sewn together as opposed to assembling them by coiling. Multiple-strand jutes are used for core material. All strands can be wrapped for thick portions, then some of the strands separated to achieve thinner sections.

BRAIDED BASKET. Dona Meilach. 9 inches high, 5-inch diameter. Red rug yarn over multiple-strand jute. One-hundred-strand jute was separated in portions and three groups of strands wrapped separately. These strands were then braided for the basket side. Two sets of unevenly separated strands were wrapped, then the thin one snaked around the thick one for the handle. The remaining core strands were separated at the back and allowed to protrude.

SPIRAL OPTIC (detail). Louise Robbins. 7 inches high, 11-inch diameter. Multiple-colored basket employs the Lazy Squaw stitch. The coils are wrapped in different colors; some extend beyond the basic basket shape and create negative spaces; others project out and around. In some areas two colors of yarn are wrapped simultaneously.

HELMET. Gwynne Lott. Red, orange, and gold fibers over jute. Inspired by native Peruvian wool hats and created with basketry techniques and wrapping. *Opposite:* Details: (*left*) Two thick wrapped cores project from the center top. (*right*) The interior.

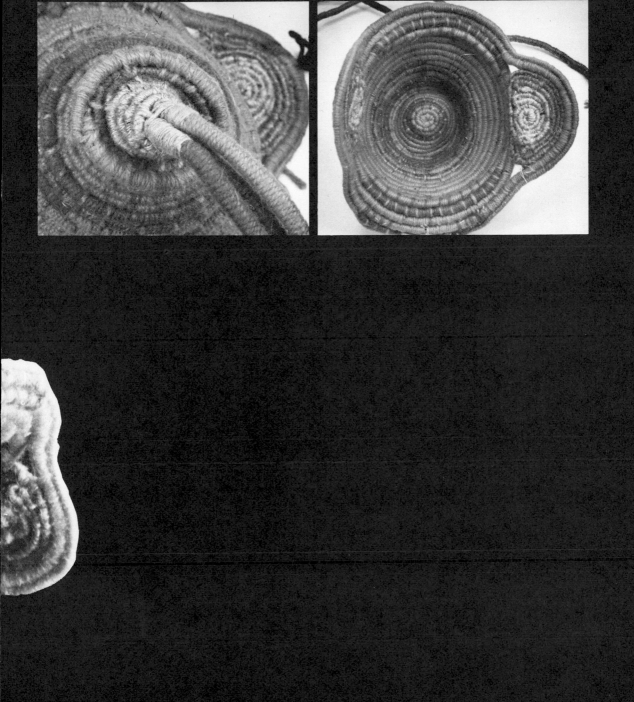

MORE WAYS TO BEGIN A COIL

In addition to the traditional coil center already demonstrated, other ways to begin a coil are illustrated.

1. Tie an overhand knot; place a needle on one strand.

2. Bring the needle through the center of the knot.

3. Use the three strands for the core and the fourth strand as the wrapping material. Begin with a longer piece than shown, add core and weft as needed.

4. Begin coil with a large bead at the center. Or, if a traditionally made center is not tightly pulled, stitch a bead into the hole later, if desired.

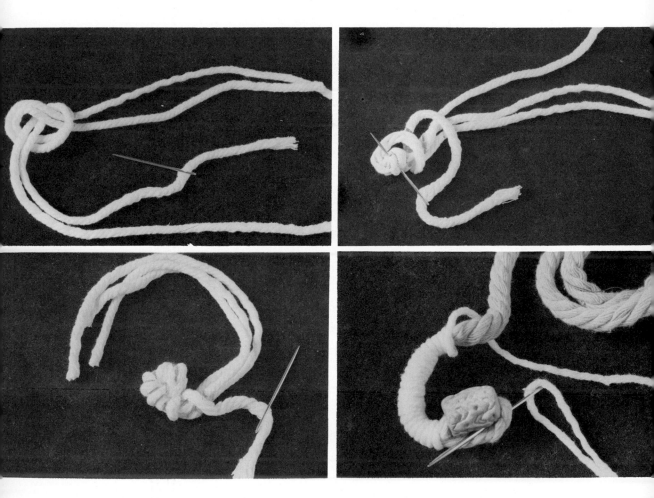

The Chinese Crown Knot appears in the center of baskets made by the Chinese (see page 17 for an example), and an adaptation of it was used by the Salish Indians, who tied it over a core of wood. Use two threads woven together as shown. (*Note:* The first two steps are illustrated with different-type cords for clarity. In use, use two or more cords of the same weight.) (a) Place the left cord with two opposing bends. (b) Wind the right cord through the bends of the left cord from the top in the direction of the arrows. It goes *under* the top cord, then *over* the next two. Bend it and go back *under* all three. Bend again and bring it down *over* two cords, *under* one, and tighten. (c) The finished knot; use one strand for wrapping around the others that naturally form the core as in the Overhand Knot Wrap, page 87.

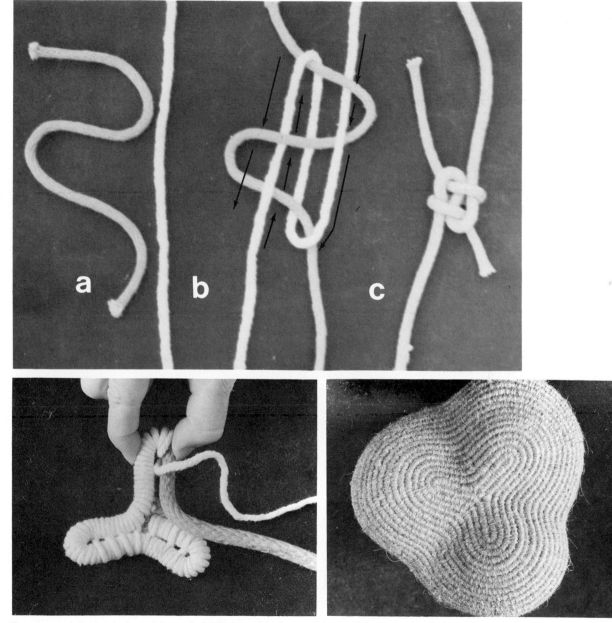

The shape of the beginning of the coil determines the shape of the basket. A cloverleaf shape at right is begun by wrapping the center, as shown. Kathy Malec.

IMBRICATION

Imbrication is another method for adding color and texture to a basket surface. It can be accomplished while you are coiling by folding an extra strip of material along the core and catching it in with the weft. It can also be added on over a completed coil. It is especially effective with yarn or a broad material such as a strip of raffia or ribbon. Imbricated baskets are sometimes called "klikitat" after a tribe that used the technique to produce rectangular block designs on the surfaces of their forms. But only tall, narrow, imbricated baskets are unique to this tribe: many other tribes and peoples do imbrication. The added color appears only on the outside of the basket and not on the inside. The technique can also be applied to twined and crocheted work.

1. The first row of imbrication shows the added thread folded and placed under the weft.

2. For the adjacent row, the weft is brought down and connected to the weft of the previous row.

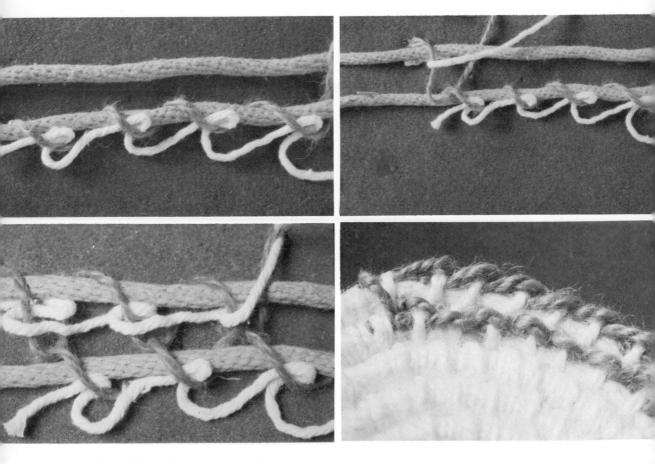

3. The folding and overlapping continue.

4. Two coils with brown imbricated under white weft. A broader added color will completely hide the coil and result in a square pattern. Or the folded materials may be allowed to project so they form a design.

BASKET WITH IMBRICATION. Stana Coleman. 3 inches high, 4-inch diameter. Wool with rawhide strips added in the imbricated method. You can observe how the folded rawhide protrudes for a motif.

Chinese Basket (detail). The imbricated folds have been woven into with an extra piece of cane for an additional surface decoration.

THE BUTTONHOLE OR BLANKET STITCH

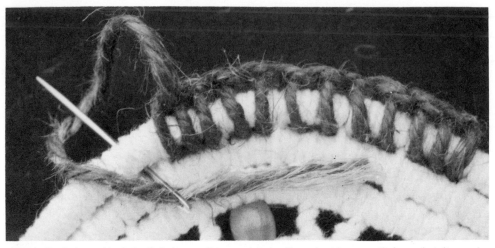

The buttonhole or blanket stitch is usually associated with embroidery or stitchery; but it can be applied to the edge of a basket for a decorative finish. The stitches may be placed close together or far apart. They can be accomplished as you wrap a core fiber, or added over a previously wrapped coil. You may also wrap a length of core with the stitch and then sew it to a finished basket edge in a design, as illustrated below.

To do the stitch, insert your needle between the coils; leave a loop, as shown. Then bring your needle up and through the loop. Pull tightly. The result will be a ridge which you may have to manipulate so it sits on the edge of the coil neatly.

Ethiopian Coiled Basket (detail). Buttonhole stitch trims edges of outer coils. Approximately 10 inches in diameter.

Collection, Joan Austin,
San Diego, California

Traditional Indian baskets sometimes have a detail showing how one weft stitch has split the stitch below it. This is easily accomplished when multiple strands of easy-to-split grasses are used. A similar effect can be accomplished by using two or more strands of weft with a Lazy Squaw stitch. As you coil the strands, place your needle so it splits the threads in the stitch of each preceding row. The detail can be worked onto portions of the basket or throughout. It can also be added onto the completed basket as an embroidered detail.

The Lazy Squaw stitch has been split as it is made on each subsequent row (detail). Stana Coleman.

Or make some of the Lazy Squaw stitches over two or more rows, planning them so they are close together or far apart, as desired.

EMBROIDERY

Many Indian and Mexican baskets are decorated with a technique called "false embroidery." As the coiling or twining progresses, a colored strand is twisted around each weft and shows only on the surface of the basket. Modern artists have shortcutted this method and opt for straight embroidery methods to decorate a basket. These might include stitches that go through the basket, as in needlepoint, so that the stitch appears on inside and outside surfaces, or it can be accomplished so it appears only on the outside.

BROWN JUTE BASKET. Joyce Barnes. 9 inches high, 5-inch diameter. The Figure Eight stitch is combined with long and short lengths of Lazy Squaw stitches worked into a pattern that is developed as the basket is constructed, or added later as an embroidered stitch. Observe the "hinged" lid.

Mexican Basket. Hidalgo State. 16 inches high, 12 inches wide, 6 inches deep. Coiled with color painted on and some stitched details over the coils.

PEOPLE BASKET. Barbara Kincaid. 5 inches high, 3½-inch diameter. Facial features, arms, bows for hats, and some beading are added to the coiled basket made of novelty yarns over jute cores.

TIZOC, MIGHTY WARRIOR. Jan Cohen. Mexican sisal over a jute core. Nose, eyes, brows, ears, and other appurtenances are added with additional coiling, embroidery, and sewing.

Courtesy, artist

KNOTLESS NETTING OR LOOPING

A looping stitch, also called "knotless netting" by weavers, is frequently used for entire baskets, between coils, or as a motif over coils. Once you perfect the simple technique, use it innovatively wherever you like. The examples illustrated employ stiff fibers such as rattan and kelp. These materials are dampened so they can be manipulated into the necessary loops. You can develop the same motif in jute, sisal, and other stiff fibers.

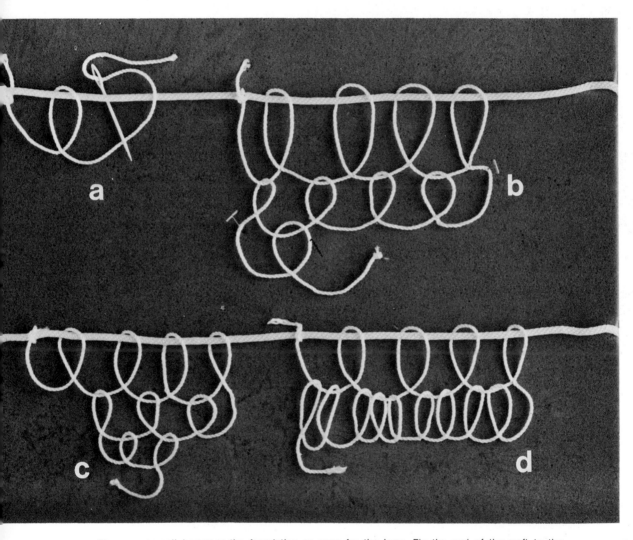

a. The core or coil becomes the foundation or warp for the loop. Fix the end of the weft to the core. To loop, bring the working thread over the core, swing to the left and under the core, then over the first part of the weft. Continue making these loops around the basket for several rows.

b. To make several rows of loops on one coil, interconnect by looping the second row over the bottom loop of the previous row. Or work it over another coil.

c. To decrease, omit working into the end loop or anywhere in the center.

d. To increase, place two or more loops on the curve of the loop in the previous row.

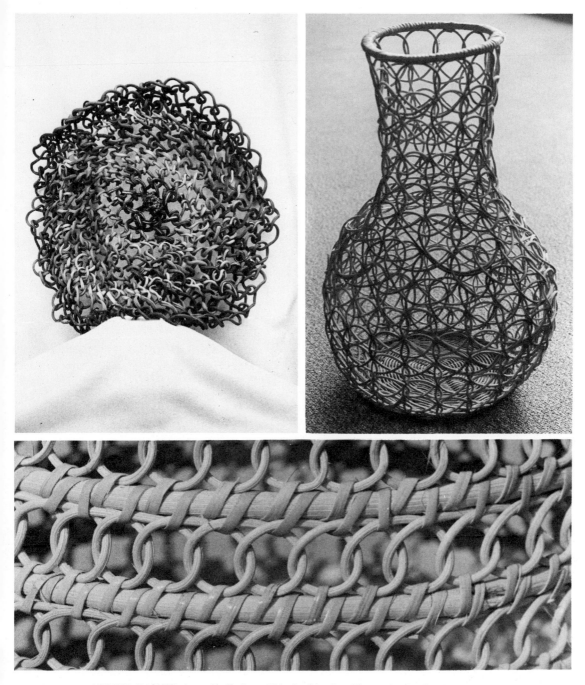

LOOPED BASKET. Lucy H. Traber. 20-inch diameter. The entire basket is interconnected looping; no coiling core is used.

Courtesy, artist

African Basket. Contemporary. 18 inches high. A woven base changes pattern and the cane is worked completely in the looped or knotless netting method.

Basket (detail). Philippines. A variation with each loop interlooped and attached to the coil by wrapping.

Collection, Dona Meilach

EXPOSED CORE

Another structural and decorative motif used in coiling is to leave portions of the core material exposed in equal or unequal lengths. The exposed core may be reeds, grasses, wood, or fibers. When soft unspun materials are used for the core material, a tightly wound weft, even though it is of fibers, will result in a solid basket. In modern basketry, when utility is not a factor, a solid basket is not always a requirement.

Exposed-core materials may be used to blend perfectly or contrast with the weft. Using an exposed-core approach results in a finished basket more quickly than wrapping every inch of core, and often it is a wise way to begin a project when time and patience are at a minimum.

Philippine Basket. 10-inch diameter. The effective use of a bundled core of cane exposed through the contrasting weft.

Collection, Stana Coleman, Evanston, Illinois

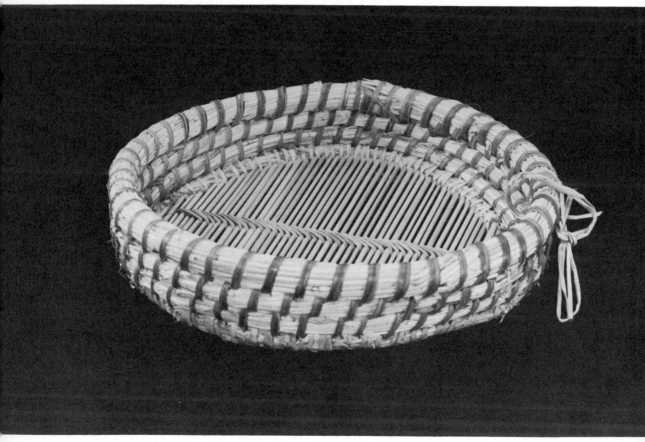

COILED BASKET. Joan Sterrenburg. Woven fibers coiled in a checkered effect exhibit the exposed core concept for its design.

Collection and courtesy, Evansville Museum of Arts and Science, Evansville, Indiana

SANTA BARBARA BIRD BASKET (detail). Debbie F. Dunn. 7 inches high, 16½-inch diameter. A core of natural reed wrapped with raffia and fiber weft. The exposed core serves as a unifying texture and color under the different weft materials.

BASKET (detail). Kathy Malec. Gray unspun jute is the exposed core material for tightly pulled gray horse-hair in a Figure Eight stitch.

American basket of a coiled bundle of oak splits with stripped wood weft.
Collection, Joan Sterrenburg, Bloomington, Indiana

RED OVOID. Jean Singerman-Weiss. 26 inches high, 15½-inch diameter. Dyed red raffia and rayon over a dyed sisal core. All colors are red, but the textured sisal exposed core contrasts with the raffia weft and rayon wrapped protruding elements.

Courtesy, artist

ADDED ELEMENTS

When creating baskets, it is important to study the existing baskets for construction methods. There is no purist approach to contemporary basket designs, and the method used is acceptable so long as it arrives at the result you want. Often, baskets with hanging parts, with multiple coils, with beads or other decorations, confuse the beginner who thinks these are all incorporated into the design as it progresses. Elements can be added by poking, lacing, or sewing them between coils or around stitches. They might be of the same, a similar, or a completely different material and color. The basket may rely more on the added element for its design than on the basket form itself. The added element may then be treated by wrapping or by knotting or with beads, crochet, feathers, or the like. To stiffen added fibers, wrap in a length of wire or clip the cords to shape and spray with starch or hair spray.

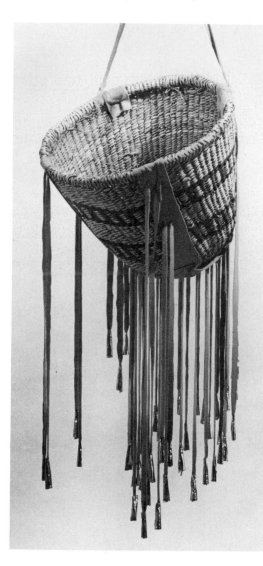

Indian Burden Basket. Twining technique. A perfect example of the application of added elements. Rawhide strips have been added onto the outside of the basket and laced along the bottom. Decorative metal endings have been pinched onto the strips to weight them.
Collection, Stana Coleman, Evanston, Illinois

BIRD-NEST BASKET. Dona Meilach. 12 inches high, 3-inch diameter. Linen weft over a cotton clothesline core. Extra strands of linen were put through the coils with a needle. An extra length of core material was added to the handle and assembled with Figure Eight wrapping. A ceramic bird dangles at the bottom.

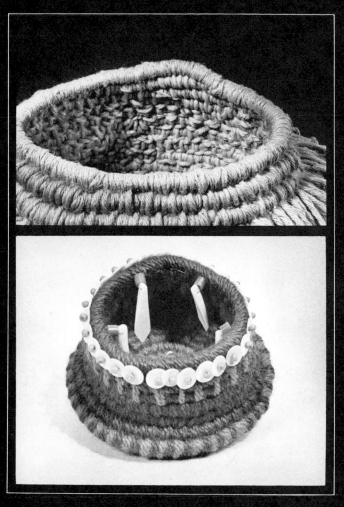

JUTE BASKET (detail). Gary Trentham. The interior illustrates how the jute strands are placed between the coils so they extend to the exterior.

BEADED BASKET. Stana Coleman. 2½ inches high, 4-inch diameter. Different shades of doubled strands of red yarn are worked in the Lazy Squaw split stitch; some stitches are carried over two coils. Beads and pieces of sliced bone have been added along the top inside and out.

<

BASKET FORM. Gary Trentham. 11 inches high, 7-inch diameter. Coiled with strands added between the elements. The strands were partially unraveled and knotted along the length and at the end.

FAT LADY. Carol Danley. Approximately 12 inches high. Raffia over cotton rope. Various parts have been assembled to create the finished figure. At left, two small baskets are shaped and stitched together. The arms and breasts are also separate shapes sewn to the body.

ASSEMBLING PARTS

Many of the baskets illustrated consist of one or more separate parts combined to form a larger shape. It is often difficult to make the coils behave in the sizes and forms desired, especially when you want large and small pieces and protrusions. Therefore, the technique is to decide how many parts you visualize for a finished piece, make them, and assemble them.

Parts can be fabricated of different materials and colors or they can be the same materials, depending upon the problems involved. It is no different than the traditional concept of adding handles that may be made separately, but appear to be part of the whole. Lids, of course, must be made separately and usually are free from the bottom portion, although in some cases they are hinged.

Parts can be assembled by coiling one portion to another, by stitching, knotting, sewing, or whatever works.

FAT LADY. Carol Danley. When the top is placed on the bottom, the figure form emerges.

COILED VESSEL. Ferne Jacobs. 6½ inches high. Synthetic and metallic yarns over waxed linen core. The top and bottom portions were coiled. Open loops were planned at the edges of the bottom section and the base of the top section. These were combined with a core wrapped with shiny metallic thread. This connecting cord was stitched together in places to give the small form greater solidity.

Courtesy, artist

SIDNEY. Lucele Coutts. 7 inches high, 16 inches wide, 8 inches deep. Rug wool on a jute coil with wood beads. Figure Eight stitch with rya knots added. Several parts assembled.

Courtesy, artist

HATCHED EGG UNDER BASKET. Virginia H. Barber. Wool weaving yarns over a jute core with feathers. Two pedestal-shaped basket forms hold a fibre-coiled egg that is made in two parts and hinged.

Courtesy, artist

Above:

THE FRESNO BEE. Frank Kong. 6 inches high, 14½ inches wide. Raffia wrapped over a 20-gauge wire core with a Lazy Squaw stitch. Lightweight yellow and green fabric is inlaid between the wrapped wires for the insect's wings.

Courtesy, artist

Below:

CHARLEY'S DREAM. Frank Kong. 4 inches high, 9 inches wide, 10 inches deep. Raffia over a 20-gauge wire core. Lazy Squaw stitch.

Courtesy, artist

THE QUIET CLASSROOM. Frank Kong. 12 inches high, 12 inches wide. Natural raffia over 20-gauge wire core attached to the doll heads.

Courtesy, artist

UNTITLED. Frank Kong. 8 inches high, 8 inches wide. Raffia over a 20-gauge wire core. The ends are stitched into holes made at the top of the doll legs.

Courtesy, artist

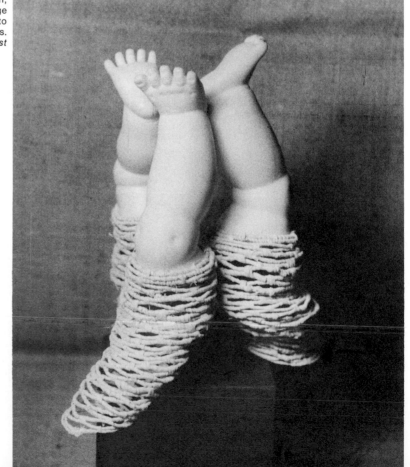

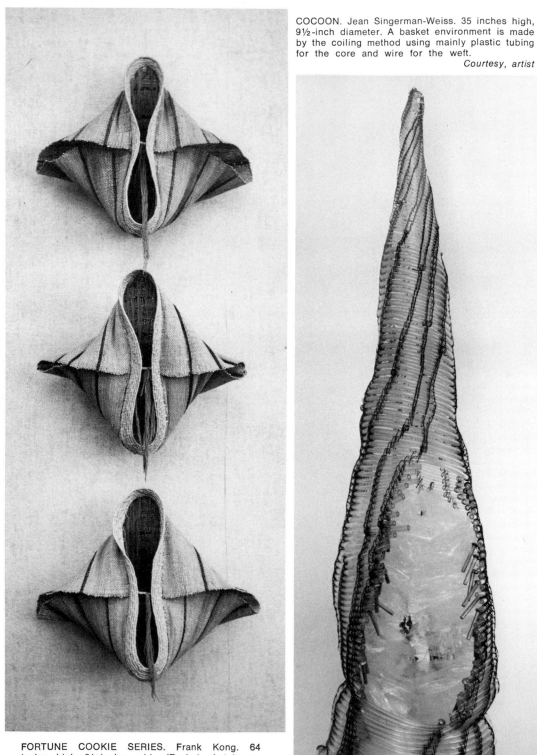

COCOON. Jean Singerman-Weiss. 35 inches high, 9½-inch diameter. A basket environment is made by the coiling method using mainly plastic tubing for the core and wire for the weft.

Courtesy, artist

FORTUNE COOKIE SERIES. Frank Kong. 64 inches high, 21 inches wide. (Each basket is approximately 20 inches high.) The main portion of each fortune cookie is woven on a floor loom using cotton raffia. Lazy Squaw coiling edges the centers.

Courtesy, artist

WALL HANGING. Jean Lamon. Coiling with acrylic painted on the surface for hardness and sheen.
Courtesy, artist

WALL HANGING. Geoff Welch. 6 feet high, 2 feet wide. Leather, formed while wet, has been combined with spun horsehair, horse tail, and bone. The fibers are coiled and attached to the leather.
Courtesy, artist

MASK. Eileen Bernard. Primitive peoples often used basketry methods for ritual masks. Eileen Bernard uses this same idea for interpreting a primitive mask into modern materials and concepts.
Photo, Lee Snadow

DAVID'S CLASS. Frank Kong. 18 inches high. Natural raffia over a twisted paper core. The eyes and mouth are crocheted.
Courtesy, artist

Crested mask of the Mmwo society (cult of female ancestral spirits). Ibo, Nigeria. A wood mask inspired the design above. Portions of a primitive piece can be used for developing basket trims, designs, and for other masks.
Courtesy, The British Museum, London

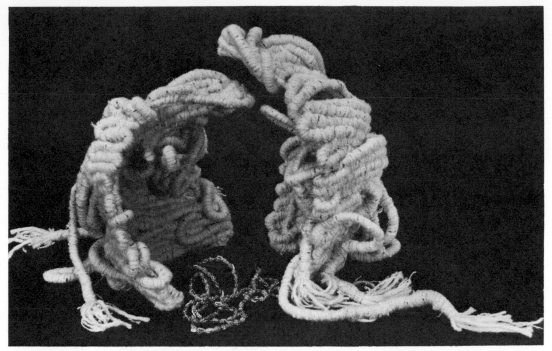

UNTITLED. Ruby Conaway Lassanyi. 13 inches high, 16 inches wide, 12 inches deep. Two-part environment of coiled cotton suggests a cave with objects from the sea to form an environmental sculpture.

BASKET SCULPTURE. Susan Stroll. 8 inches high, 9 inches wide, 7 inches deep. Raffia over a sisal core in a free-form shape.

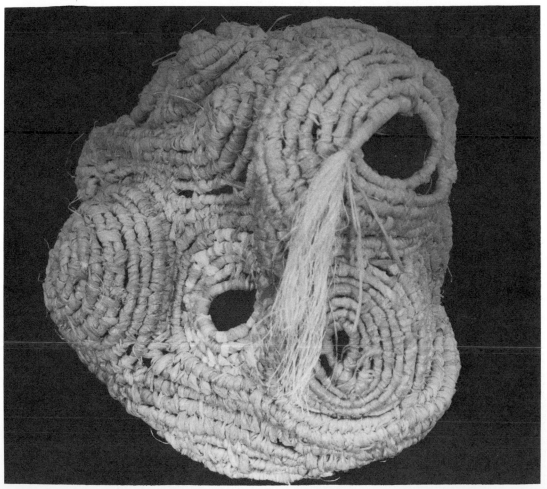

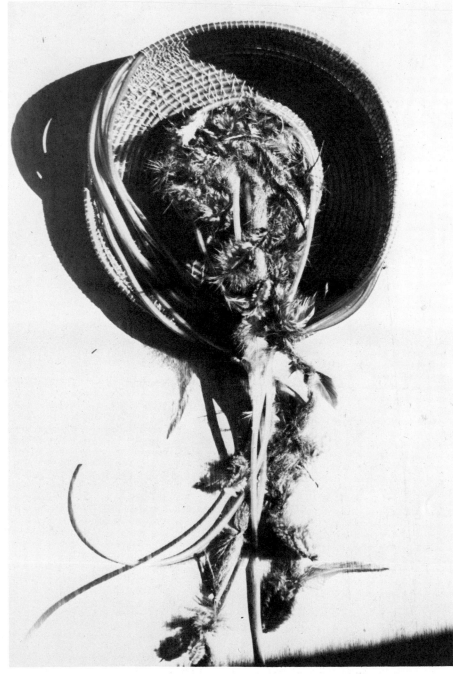

NAVEL. Gloria Bornstein. Coiled basketry technique with upholsterer's thread over a rubber tubing core. Feathers added.

Photo, Lee Sims

<

UNTITLED. Jan Mjelde Wader. 29 inches high, 14 inches wide, 1½ inches deep. Raffia over a reed core with feathers added.

A GALLERY OF BASKETRY EXAMPLES

In addition to the examples already shown for coiling, the follow-ing are offered to illustrate the varied directions that modern basketry forms are taking. The shapes, materials, and their combinations may be used to stimulate original and inventive concepts.

QUICKENING. Libby Platus. 30-inch diameter. Figure Eight and Lazy Squaw stitches are used for the bottom. The rolled side and top are Clove Hitching. Horsehair is a stitched-on added element.

Courtesy, artist

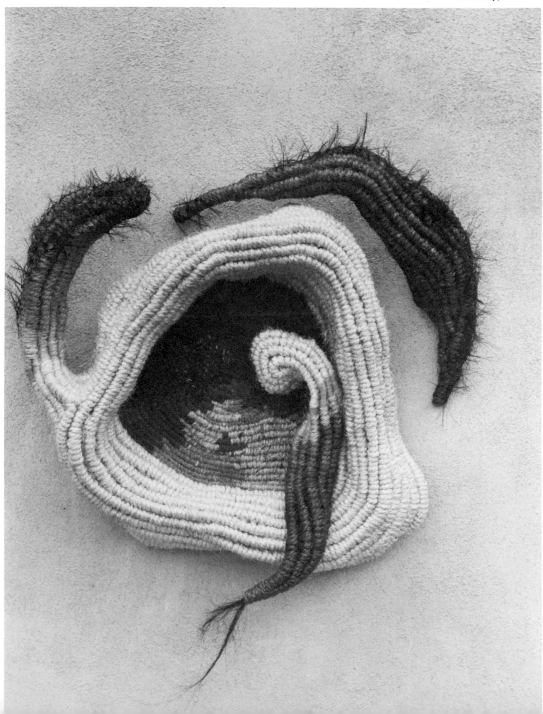

Eileen Bernard. Lace Stitch is used with coiled basketry techniques to create a lamp. The piece is worked over a lampshade frame and the interior is fitted with a socket. When turned on, light shines between the coils and a God's Eye woven top permits an interesting cast shadow on the ceiling.

Photo, Lee Snadow

WIRE BASKET. Bonnie Zimmer. 12½ inches high, 10 inches wide. Screen-wire mesh, rolled into tubes, was coiled and held together by improvised methods including twining and Figure Eight stitching.

>

WOVEN-STUFFED BASKET. Gary Trentham. 21 inches high, 14-inch di-ameter. Chartreuse linen and rayon tubes were woven on a loom. Each tube, about four inches wide, was stuffed and sewn together in a coillike manner.

BASKET. Gyongy Laky. Plastic casing stuffed with fibers including sisal, straw, and packing materials and held together with fishing line in Figure Eight and Lazy Squaw stitches.
Photographed at the Richmond Art Center, Richmond, California

OSAGE APPLE BASKET. Stana Coleman. Purple wool over a jute core. Lazy Squaw and some Lace stitches between coils. A green crochet stuffed form is placed within to represent an apple. The trim is made of bone slices with beads.

BIRD NEST. Sue Brown. 5 inches high, 9½-inch diameter. An off-centered shape with different thicknesses of cores. Cores are composed of multiple strands of raffia, and the weft is brown and black raffia. Feathers nestle inside the basket.

Opposite:
COILED CONTAINER WITH EGG
FORM. Ferne Jacobs. 6 inches
high, 4-inch diameter plus egg.
Multicolored yarns and natural
linen.

Courtesy, artist

MT. TAM SUN. Gayle Luchessa.
24 inches high, 7-inch diameter
at base. Gray, maroon, orange,
yellow, and pink wool over a jute
core. Some added stitchery and
beads.

SEUSS POTS (open views). Gayle Luchessa. Many of the baskets illustrated throughout the book are made in two parts. The top is carefully fabricated so it has a lip or other device that fits into or onto the base. These pots by Mrs. Luchessa are English mohair and linen over a cotton roving core.

PINK, PURPLE, RED. Helen Hennessey. 11 inches high, 6-inch diameter. Various wools worked in the Figure Eight stitch. Beads and feathers added. The top is made like a stopper cork.

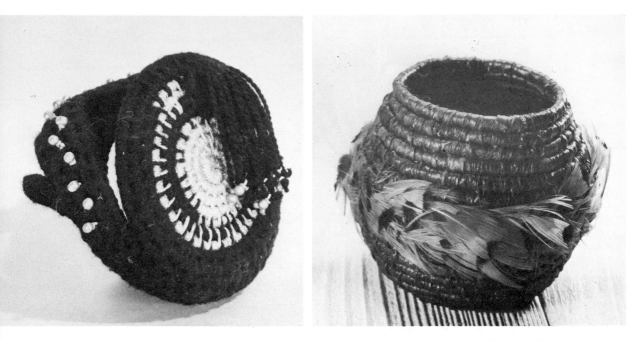

BASKET FORM. Stana Coleman. 4 inches high, 6-inch diameter. A pattern of silver metallic thread has been worked into the bottom of the basket to complement the composition.

FEATHERED POMO. Eileen Bernard. 6 inches high, 6-inch diameter. Raffia over a jute core with feathers.

FEATHERED BASKET. Marie Waters. 3 inches high, 8-inch diameter. Lace stitch in natural raffia on a jute core with pheasant feathers.

Courtesy, artist

SCULPTURAL BASKET. Linda Ann Valeri. (*left*) 6 inches high, 4-inch diameter. Black and white mohair with black and white pheasant feathers. (*right*) SMALL HANGING BASKET. Linda Ann Valeri. 4 inches high, 2½-inch diameter. Reindeer yarn, guinea hen feathers, and beads.

UNTITLED. Pat Williams. 14 inches high, 12 inches wide, 1½ inches deep. Fine linen over a jute core. The concept of assembling several basket shapes is illustrated in this wall hanging. The three basket forms at the top protrude while the large bottom shape is concave. When the piece is reversed, the opposite occurs. Coils from each section are combined to hold the parts together. It is finished with wrapping and fringed elements.

UNTITLED. Joan Austin. Approximately 14 inches high, 8-inch diameter. Two shapes are combined. The base is made as one part with a round shape set on top much like a stemmed water goblet. The addition of feathers and wrapping completes the piece.

Courtesy, artist

BASKET FORM. Stana Coleman. 3 inches high, 4-inch diameter. Red and orange wool over a jute core. The core has been extended to form a lip; some negative shapes result. Lazy Squaw stitch.

FEATHERED FRIEND. Louise Robbins. 7 inches high, 6-inch diameter. Lazy Squaw stitch forms a pattern in earth-tone wools with colored feathers.

BASKETS. Kathy Malec. Each is 8 inches high, 9-inch diameter. The basket (*right*) is dyed with cochineal dye, which yields a reddish purple tone. Both are dyed wool over a wool roving core.

FEATHER BASKET WITH HANDLE. Suellen Glashausser. Figure Eight coiling worked with double threads over an exposed core.

Courtesy, artist

LACE-STITCH BASKET. Eileen Bernard. 14 inches high, 8-inch diameter. Rayon yarn over jute. Beads and feathers added.

Photo, Lee Snadow

FEATHERED FUNGUS. Lucele Coutts. 9 inches high, 7-inch diameter. Rug wool and knitting worsted on a fiber rush core. Figure Eight stitch with added rya knots.

Courtesy, artist

>

Wolfram Krank uses a core of reed and works it into colorful baskets using a variety of yarns and wrapping methods.
Courtesy, artist

COILED JEWELRY

BASKET NECKLACE. Eileen Bernard. Colored synthetic raffia has been cleverly worked over a raffia core and a circular wire neckband to create jewelry that is unique. Beads are added.

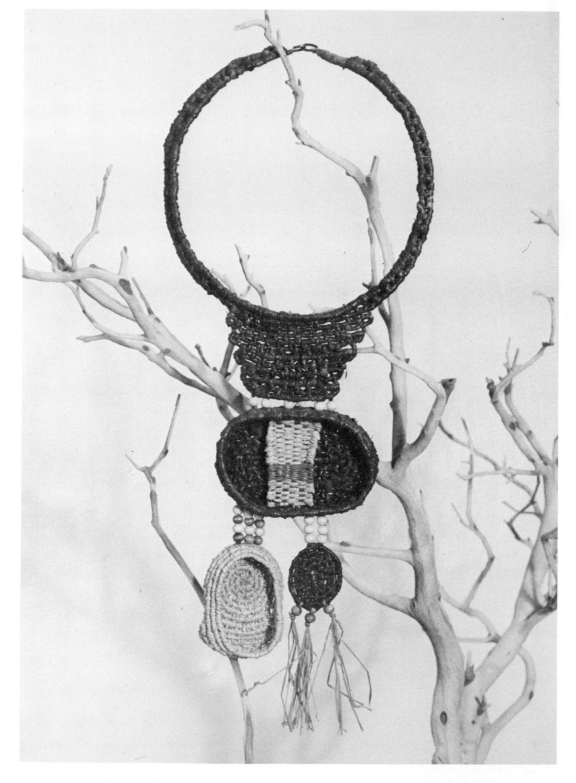

NECKPIECE. Eileen Bernard. Wool and linen using coiling and wrapping techniques over multiple-strand jute.

GOLD BRACELET. Eileen Bernard. Gold metallic yarn is used with the Lazy Squaw stitch over a fine linen core. The solid band was made first and the circular shape added on.

BELT. Eileen Bernard. Coiling methods are used to begin the end of the belt, then wrapping and a tassel complete the design.

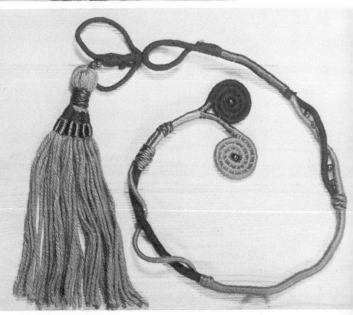

COILED NECKLACE WITH CORAL. Helen Hennessey. Dull wool and shiny curly rayon novelty
yarns are combined to form the necklace that is
adorned with coral. A circular coiled base sup-
ports the coral. Many of the wrapped strands are
sewn together rather than bound with the Figure
Eight or Lazy Squaw stitches so that one thread
does not overlap the adjacent coil.

COILED NECKLACES. Helen Hennessey. Coiling
used, as at left, and with feathers.

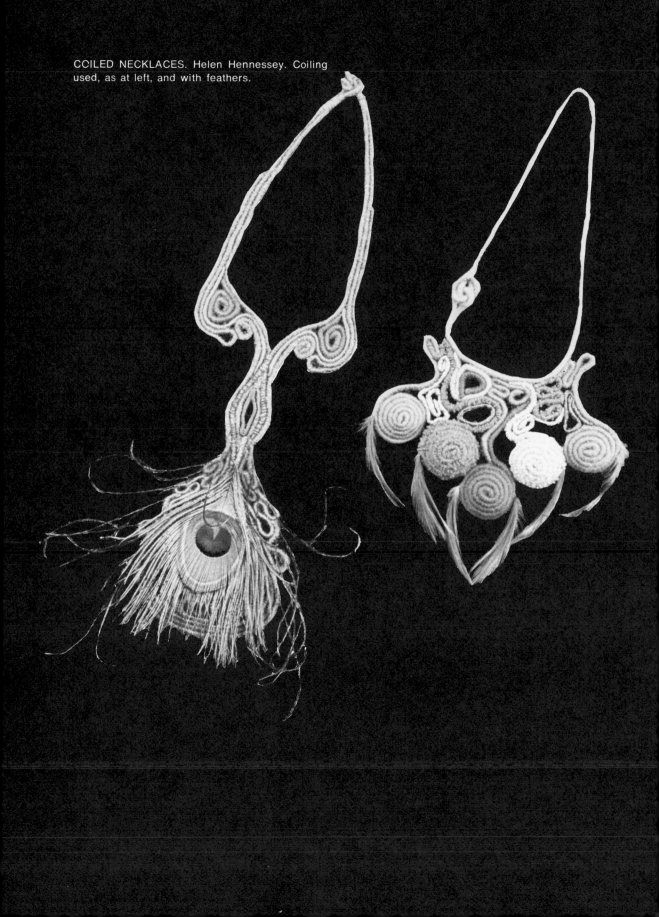

Assembling parts for a necklace involves creating the necessary shapes and then stitching them together. Some of the coils utilize conventional coiling stitches: the Figure Eight and Lazy Squaw. But when you do not wish colors to show from one coil to the next, sew the wrapped strands with clear thread or a matching color thread.

Backs of the feather necklaces (*preceding page*), by Helen Hennessey, show the intricate base for the coral (page 142) and for the peacock feather wrapped onto the necklace (page 143).

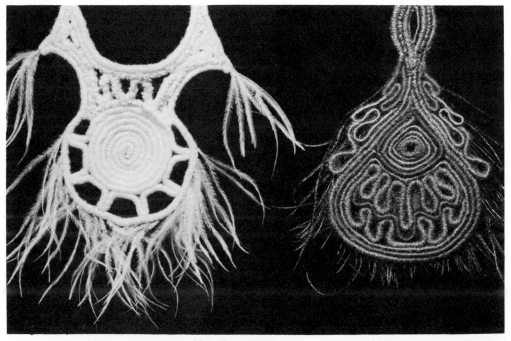

BASKET NECKLACES. Joyce Barnes. Coiling and wrapping with beads, mirrors, and stitching.

COLLAR MASK. Virginia H. Barber. Coiling,
weaving, and macramé.

Courtesy, artist   Coiled oval base for necklaces, above.

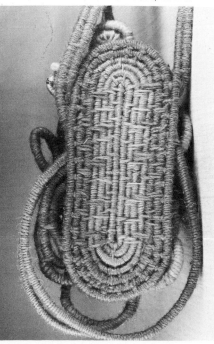

5

Twining

Twining, also called weft twining, is believed to be older than weaving, and involves at least two wefts enclosing a warp. Twining examples dating back to 2000 B.C. have been found in Peru and later throughout South America. It appears in textiles and baskets of many cultures.

The recent history of the American Indian, the Chinese, and the Africans exhibits a rich source of twining examples still used extensively in baskets made today. Once you recognize the differences in the twining pattern compared to coiling, plain weaving, and knotting, you'll have no trouble analyzing the construction of baskets.

There are several variations of simple twining, and those most often used are illustrated here. For additional variations refer to *The Primary Structures of Fabrics* by Irene Emery and to others listed in the Bibliography.

The procedure involves consistently crossing the same pair of wefts in the same way over each warp. To simplify the procedure, establish a hand movement and rhythm so that you enclose a warp, twist the wefts, and enclose the next warp, always carrying one weft over and one under the warp.

As you become adept at twining you'll understand how color can be controlled. For solid patterning, the wefts must be crossed in the same way each time. When they are crossed in opposite directions, the color rendition will have a mosaic appearance. Changing the directions of the color in a section also results in a color pattern change. Rows of different color wefts yield a striped pattern.

Twined baskets may be started from either the top or the bottom and both procedures are explained. Finishing off loose warp ends is a greater problem in twining than in coiling. In twining, you have many ends; in coiling, only one or a few. The solutions for gathering the leftover warps at top and bottom should be carefully studied. Wrapping and other ending solutions introduced for coiling are also applied to twined baskets.

<

SPRING. Molly Baross. 14 inches high, 7-inch diameter. Dyed raffia over cane. Twining. A beautiful solution for making the structural warp increases decorative, well-integrated elements (see detail, page 157).

SIMPLE TWINING AND VARIATIONS

There is not as much versatility possible in shaping a twined basket as in a coiled basket; increases and decreases are relatively static and usually are more structural than decorative. Many twined baskets are made in two or more parts and assembled. Often the artist combines twining with macramé and with woven portions, both in the basket and for finishing.

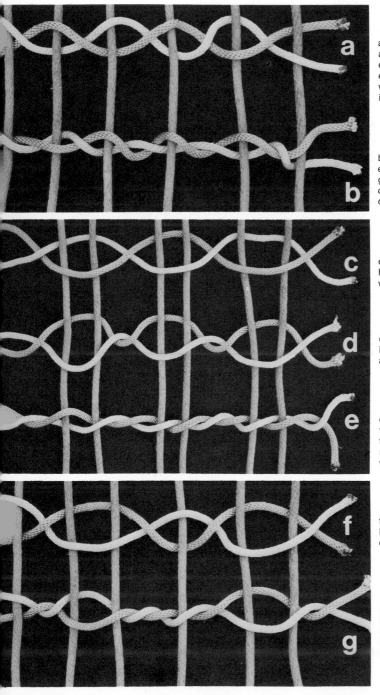

a. HALF TURN OR SINGLE TWIST: The simplest and most often used twining technique: two wefts enclose each warp. They cross once between each warp; each cord reverses its position every warp. When two colors are used, the rows result in an alternating dark and light mosaiclike pattern.

b. FULL TURN OR DOUBLE TWIST: The two wefts enclose each warp as above, BUT the wefts are given a full turn between each warp and the same cord is always on top of each warp. With two colors, the result is a row of each color.

c. PAIRED WARP, also called Paired Twining with Half Turn: Two wefts enclose each pair of warps with a half turn between each group.

d. PAIRED WARP, also called Paired Twining with Full Turn: Two wefts enclose pairs of warps with a full turn between.

e. ALTERNATE HALF TURN, FULL TURN: In this variation the wefts enclose each warp, but a half turn is used over each of two warps, then one or more full turns are made before enclosing the next warp. The pattern is repeated.

f. Another variation: Use the two wefts with the Half Turn alternating and enclosing one warp, then enclosing two warps.

g. Use the Full Turn and the Half Turn in different combinations, enclosing one and two warps. When developing a basket with the variations, you will have to carefully work out a pattern, unless you prefer a random, free design.

COMPACT TWINING: A simple Half Turn twining pattern repeated row after row in the same direction and pushed or beaten together results in a densely woven fabric that has some elasticity to it. For an even appearance, the wefts must always cross each other in the same direction in every row. This is referred to as compact twining, or as a Z twist.

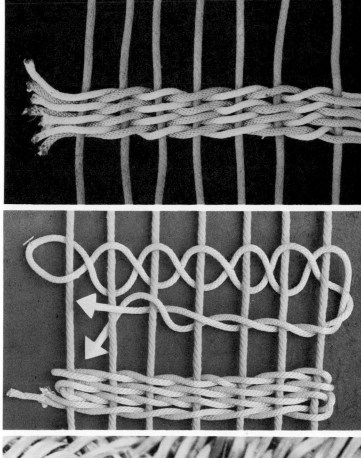

A

B

COUNTERED TWINING: When simple Half Turn twining (as above) is reversed in direction, the twist of the wefts forms a different pattern in the reverse row: Note the difference between A and B.

Detail from a twined basket by Molly Baross made of cane over cane spokes. It illustrates both compact twining and countered twining, resulting in two patterns. The cane had to be continually soaked in hot water so it was soft and pliable enough to be twined.

PEDESTAL POT (detail). Dee Nemeth. Sisal. Compact twining. All the fibers are worked in one direction: the result is slightly elastic so it will slide onto and fit snugly over a glass bowl.

HOW TO DEVELOP A TWINED BASKET

1.   There are basically two ways to begin a twined basket; each has variations. (*left*) A basket is begun from the bottom center with two sets of crossed-over squares, then it is shaped and finished at the top. (*right*) A basket is begun at the top and finished at the base.

2.   This first series of photos demonstrates the technique for beginning a basket at the base and working up. Cut two sets of warps of any number and long enough to yield the combined base and height of the basket. For illustrating, we are using two sets of three warps to begin. Three cords are pinned to a foam rubber working board. A length of weft is doubled and twined over the three cords as shown.

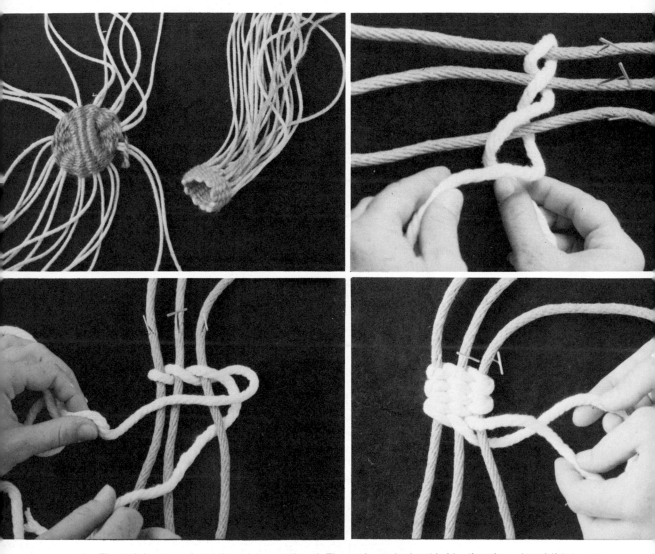

3.   The weft is returned and the twining continued. The work can be hand-held rather than pinned if it is more convenient. Flexible materials such as rope and twine usually are easier to start when they are pinned. Willow, cane, and so forth can be readily hand-held.

4.   Twine back and forth for three rows (any number of rows could be made depending on the size you want the base to be and the thickness of your cords). Make two squares the same.

5. Place one square on top of another and press together very hard, placing it on the floor and stepping on it if necessary. Use one pair of twining wefts from the top square and connect to the corner warp of the bottom square.

6. Continue to twine the weft around all twelve cords in succession. You can also use the weft from the bottom square.

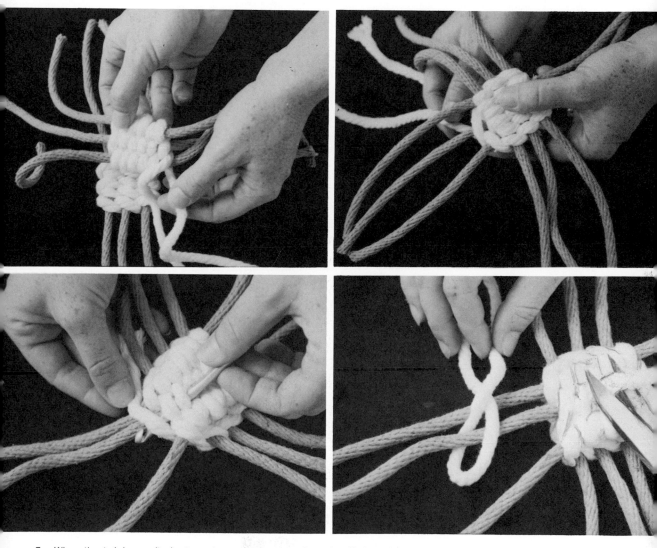

7. When the twining weft shortens, taper the loose ends and pull them into the cords with a crochet hook, or poke in with a needle or awl.

8. Double a new weft and continue to work around the cords until the base is the desired size.

INCREASING THE WARP

1. When you wish to increase the size of the base you can add new warp cords (also called spokes, in basketry terms). Place one at each "corner" of the basket if you want the basket to expand evenly. For free-form shapes, add only two warps at this point, and perhaps two later on. This will throw the symmetry off balance and result in an odd shape.

2. Continue to work the weft cords around the original twelve cords plus the new four warps. Pull the weft very tightly so it really holds in the additions. If necessary, the added cords can be stitched in.

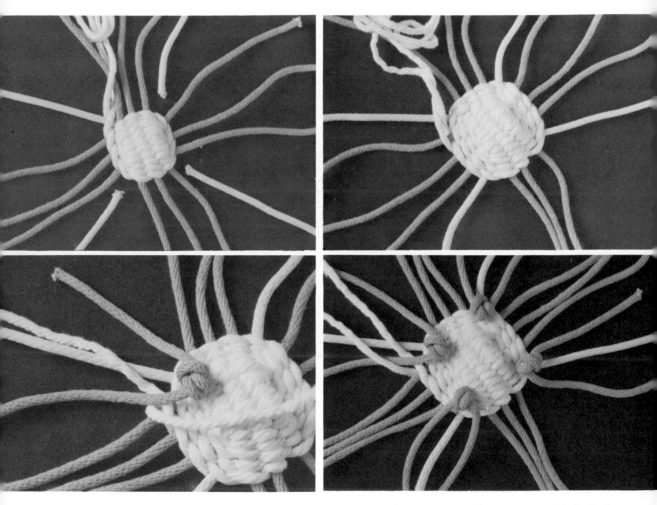

3. You can create additional warps and provide a decorative motif simultaneously. A new warp cord is knotted at the center; the knot will become a foot for the basket as well as an increase element.

4. Four knots are placed on the basket bottom with each leg placed around the first increase spoke. All the warps must be worked into the twining. There are now twenty-four cords and the original diameter of the base has been quickly doubled.

1. A bent cord wrapped for a short distance can be added in the same way. Later, you could hang a bead, a feather, or additional cords from this added element.

2. The addition might include a bead for a foot. The doubled cord is wrapped to hold the bead in place; it serves as decoration and for utility.

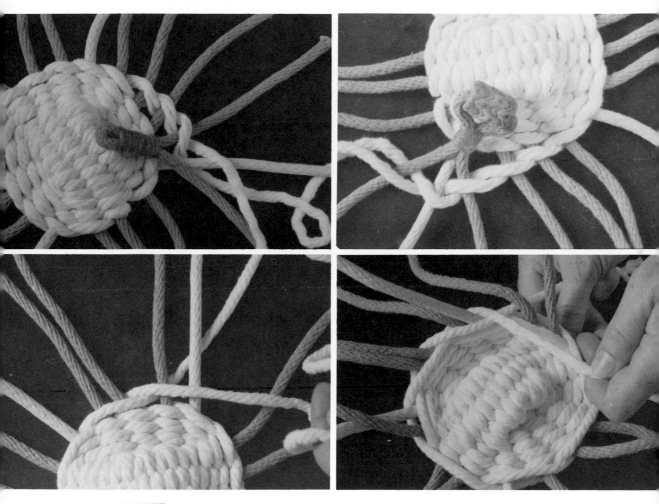

SHAPING THE BASKET

3. In twining, shaping the basket for an upward turn is accomplished by decreasing. You simply twine over two or more warps at a time, depending upon how quickly you wish the shape to change. Pull the twining weft tightly to execute the shape desired.

4. Several rows are completed and the side takes shape by twining over two warps at a time. The warp cords will protrude.

FINISHING

1. The basket continues to take shape: Its solidity will depend on the cords used and how tightly the weft is twined. The problem of finishing off the warp ends of the basket must be grappled with.

2. When the twined weft encloses two warps the top will look like this, and one must be inventive about securing the warps so the weft will be held in place.

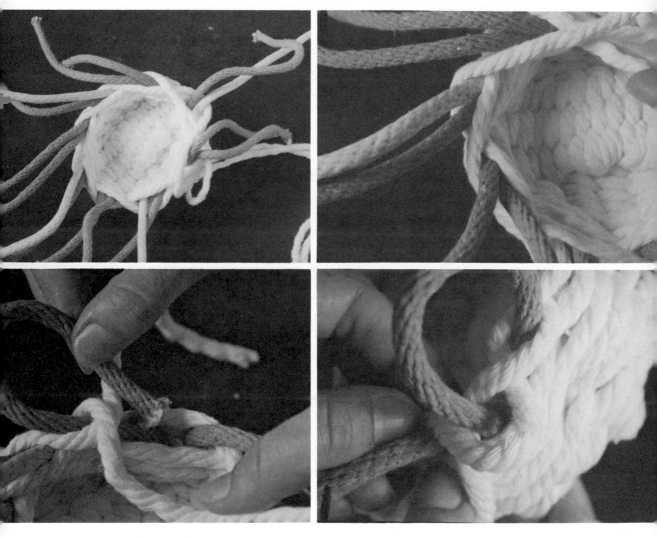

3. The traditional method for finishing a twined basket is to take one warp at a time and bend it over next to the adjacent one or two warps, overlapping each warp as you go. The resulting loop in the warp secures the weft.

4. The warp is bent and pushed back into the twined weft. It is at this point that the modern basketmaker has the freedom of creativity. Examples in this chapter, especially, should be studied to observe solutions for finishing a twined basket.

If you wish to add a handle or other element to the basket it should be pre-planned and placed under and in with the twining. The handle cords can be wrapped, braided, knotted, and so forth.

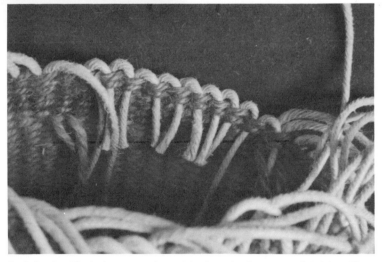

Basket edge illustrates warps turned back under two rows of twining. They may be left as is, or they can be tucked under more rows of twining and trimmed. Pulling them down tightly against the weft secures them. But one could allow the loops to extend above the weft, then lace another material through the loops before pulling them tightly down under the wefts. The ends can be stitched or glued; tapes or other material can be placed over them. Cane and reed tend to stay in without additional treatment because the tension inherent in the material makes them taut in their new position.

MORE WAYS TO BEGIN A BASE

1. Individual warps may be woven and then worked around with a weft. Do not begin the weft at the corner lest a hole result.

2. The weaving cords should be close together when you are actually working the basket. They are separated in the photo for clarity.

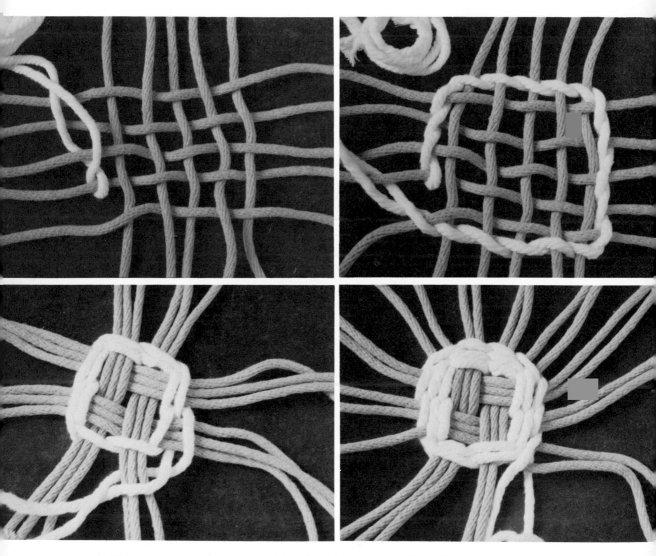

3. Multiples of cords can be woven and then the twining developed to hold them together.

4. A woven base is expanded by adding warps, or spokes, as needed, in the same way as in the double-square base.

SPRING (detail). Molly Baross. Raffia twined over reeds. The base was developed by overlapping the central reeds as in the conventional double-square manner. Additional reeds were added on the outside instead of trying to camouflage them between the warps or on the inside. They created a pattern, they accomplished the increase necessary, and provided the viewer with an insight into the intricacies required for shaping a basket. (The entire piece is illustrated on page 146.)

HANGING BASKET. Linda Ann Valeri. 11 inches high, 4-inch diameter. The base begins from overlapped reeds in the double square and is twined with raffia. Handles and other added elements utilize camel's hair yarn, rabbit fur, and pheasant feathers. Wooden beads are placed on the reed warp ends for a finishing solution. When expanding a shape, observe that the twining is worked more loosely than in the narrow sections.

Twined baskets in progress. Joan Austin. (*left*) A woven base of ash strips is twined with yarn. Thick reeds form the legs and an increase. A round basket can be accomplished from a square base when the increases are added carefully. In the basket (*right*) doubled knotted cords accomplish the addition at the base and around the sides; they also provide a decorative element.

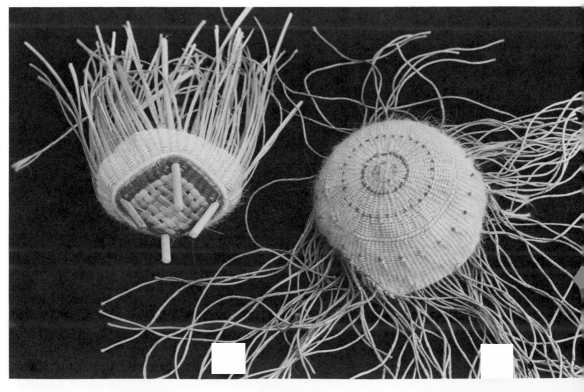

UNTITLED. Molly Baross. 8 inches high, 5-inch diameter. Unspun sisal is twined over cane. The basket was dyed gray after it was completed. Shaping is accomplished by adding and deleting warps and by pulling the twining tighter in some areas than in others.

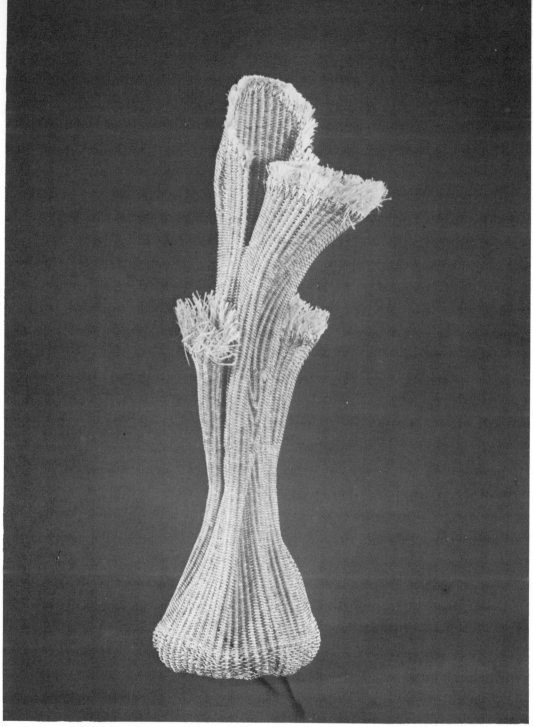

WINTER. Molly Baross. 12 inches high, 3¼-inch diameter. Metallic elastic thread twined over thin, flexible reed. Says Ms. Baross: "The metallic elastic thread gave a unique versatility. The basket took shape very easily, stretching, bending, joining, and growing in a fun way. To keep the reed limber and pliable, it was necessary to soak it in hot water, so the thread lost must of its original color, but the finished overall appearance was exciting."

WINTER (details). Molly Baross. (*above*) The double-square base beginning over four reeds also illustrates the addition of reeds to expand the shape. (*below*) The finished top was accomplished by splitting and fraying the reed; yarn was stitched around the top of the weft to secure the trimming.

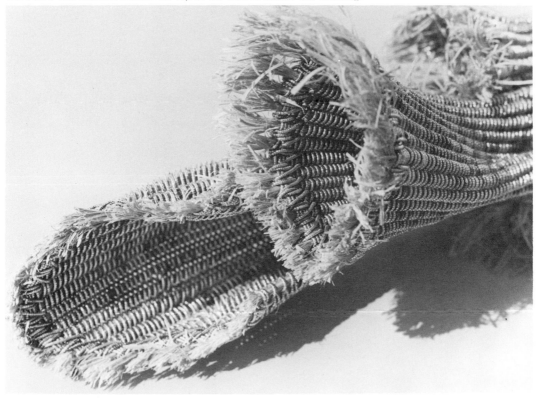

Four baskets by Pat Malarchar using a warp of 1½ lea linen and a weft of 10/5 linen. Observe the finishing techniques and how the decorative additions are also the expanding warps for the shaping.

Photos, courtesy, artist

Six inches high. Natural, black, and red. Color patterns can be developed easily using compact twining.

Four and one-half inches high. Natural and yellow linen with Indian bells on the added element, which is wrapped at top and bottom and used to expand the central portion of the basket. Where the added elements protrude at the top, the basket again decreases in diameter as at the base.

Four and one-half inches high. Natural and white. Another solution for adding warp to a twined basket.

Four and one-half inches high. Turquoise and olive linen with Indian bells.

STARTING A TWINED BASKET FROM THE TOP

The second procedure for beginning a twined basket (shown on page 150) begins by twining over looped warps that become the *top* of the basket. The problem to be solved is how to finish the base. Several solutions are shown in the examples on the following pages.

1. Cut five or more loops for warp a little longer than you wish the finished length of the basket to be. The more loops, the wider the basket. Fold the weft cord in half and place over one leg of the loop, cross, and twine over the second leg.

2. Add another looped warp and twine across each leg in turn.

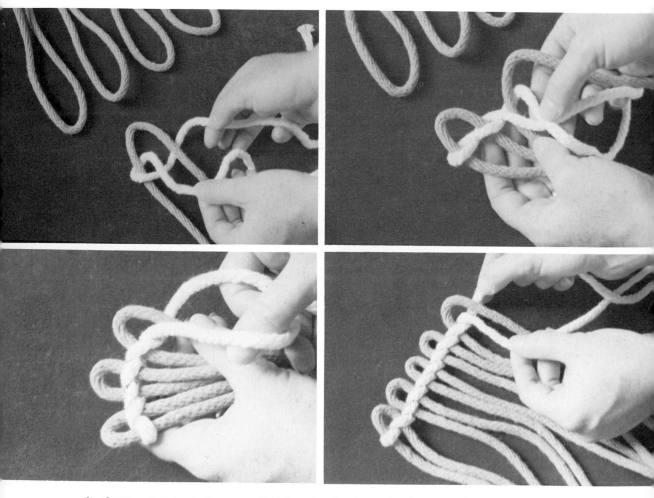

3. Continue to twine in the warps. Hold them together in one hand as you twine with the other.

4. When they are twined across all the looped warps you are ready to form the circular shape needed.

5. If you have trouble holding the warps in your hand and working, pin them to a foam rubber surface to begin.

6. Pick up first leg of the first loop and continue to twine a second row, carefully watching the crossover so it follows as you want it for compact twining. You are not returning as in countered twining, you are actually continuing in the same direction with your weft as you did in the first row.

7. Continue to twine over each warp for as many rows as you like. Pull the cords tightly for narrow sections; hold the warps on the inside and twine farther apart and more loosely for areas you wish to have bulge out.

8. Add warps by any of the methods shown on the previous pages. Here, a new loop has been knotted at the bend and added so the knot shows as a decorative element on the outside; both legs of the loop will be twined in to expand the circumference of the form.

MACRAMÉ—BEGINNING AND ENDING

1. A twined basket may be started at the top with a Lark's Head knot mounted on a length of cord (see page 192 for knotting instructions). The first row following the Lark's Head is a Vertical Clove Hitch, made with one long piece of dark cord in this example, which is also hitched over the mounting cord for a decorative beginning. Then twining is introduced.

2. For shaping, Dee Nemeth works over a beach ball. One could also use a Styrofoam form, a bowl, or a scrunched-up piece of foam rubber that could be formed into any shape.

3. Many craftsmen tend to use fringe as a purposeful ending. They exploit the leftover cords and create a decorative element from them. Dee Nemeth prefers to work the ends in so a trim, neat base results. The problem of how to secure them is overcome by the technique shown. When the basket bottom is completed (this is an open bottom that fits over a jar or is freestanding), the remaining warp cords are looped back on themselves. Then a new cord about seven times the circumference of the basket base is introduced and worked in a Vertical Clove Hitch for several rows around each looped cord.

4. To secure the loop: In the last row, the cord used for Clove Hitching is put through the loop and the loop is pulled taught. Put a dab of glue on the end to prevent it from possible pulling out at a later date. This same procedure could be used to finish the top of a basket that had been started at the base.

PEDESTAL POT (detail and finished piece). Dee Nemeth. 13 inches high, 14-inch diameter. Pot made in two parts; each part begun and ended and then assembled and placed over a glass jar. Observe the rows of Vertical Clove Hitches on the protruding sections which secure the warp endings that were mounted with a Lark's Head at the top. The base is finished the same way but cut close so no fringe remains.

UNTITLED. Dee Nemeth. 11 inches high, 15 inches wide, 11 inches deep. Macramé and twining. Sisal and jute. A free-form shape can be developed with extra circular shapes worked in.

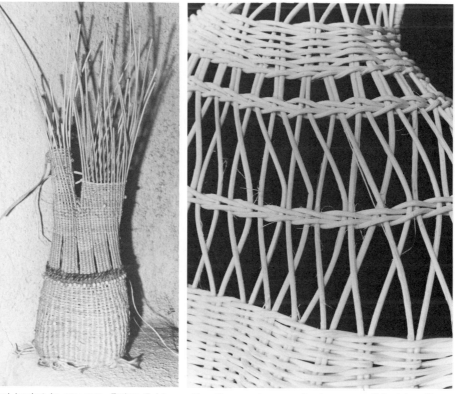

Twined basket in progress. Esther Feldman. The twining method can be used with split areas, as in weaving, to yield negative spaces.

Negative spacing can also be accomplished by allowing the warps to be exposed. Here they are crossed for added interest and strength when a stiff cane or rattan is used. A similar effect can be made with the Soumak weaving pattern (page 178).

When a basket begins at the top, finishing the bottom is a design problem. One solution is to bring the ends together and stitch them on the inside.

BASKET. Joan Austin. A square base with a round top is the result of assembling two sections and camouflaging the assembled edges with feathers. Observe how the reeds have been cut for an attractive detail.

Courtesy, artist

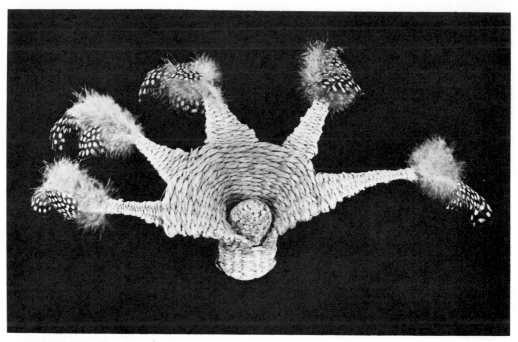

UNTITLED. Ruby Conaway Lassanyi. 8 inches high, 16 inches wide, 9 inches deep. Twined raffia with feathers and a stone inside.

BERRY BASKETS. Victoria Hill. 9 inches high, 5½-inch diameter. Baskets twined with yarns are soft and more difficult to work with than firmer warps. Crocheted fringe and stuffed berries on top.

UNTITLED. Ferne Jacobs. Twining with different color and texture wefts creates excitement in a simple shape.

UNTITLED. Stana Coleman. 7½ inches high, 4-inch diameter. Two parts are made separately and combined; the bottom is square, the top is circular. Feathers hide the bulky leftover warps wrapped within the handle.

>

HANGING BASKET. Kathy Malec. 40 inches high with fringe, 8-inch diameter. The basket is begun from the top with Square Knot sennits and two plastic rings bound in with Clove Hitches. The body is twined and the shaping shows the elasticity that results from compact twining. The bottom is completed with rings, knotting, wrapping, beads, and hanging cords.

WALL PANEL (detail). Molly Baross (see photo at right).

HANGING (detail). Kathryn McCardle (see photo at far right).

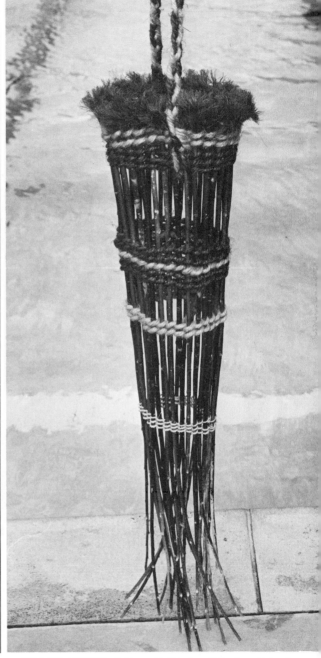

WALL PANEL. Molly Baross. 72 inches high, 8 inches deep. Unspun sisal and jute over a core of sisal rope. The piece was inspired by the twined Maori yardage woven by people of New Zealand. It illustrates how versatile twining can be for creating varied shapes.

WILLOW BASKET. Kathryn McCardle. 42 inches high, 8-inch diameter. The openness of the willow combined with sparse twined areas of jute and sisal is reminiscent of fishing baskets made by native tribes of Oceania and Africa.

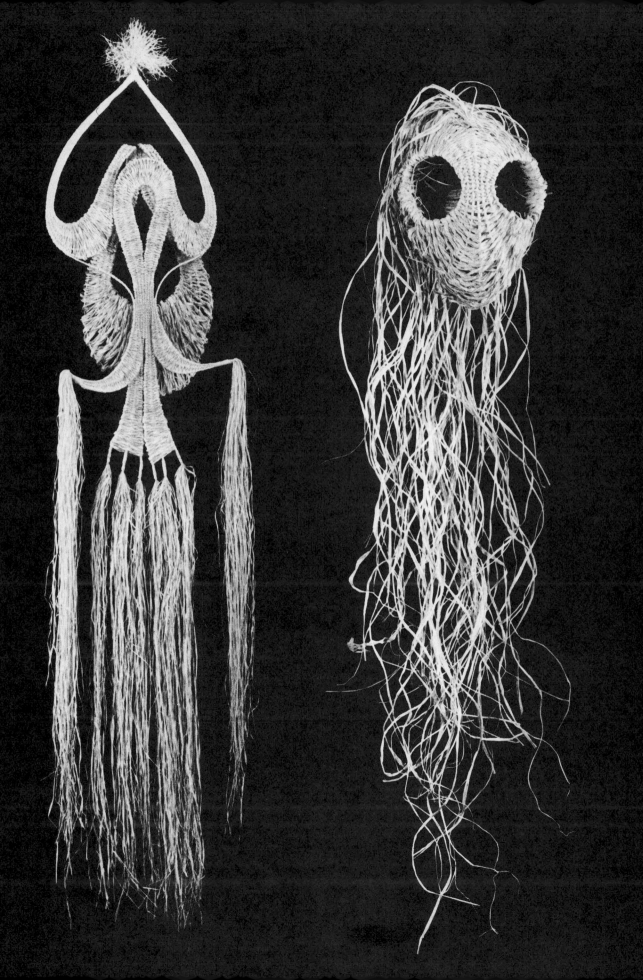

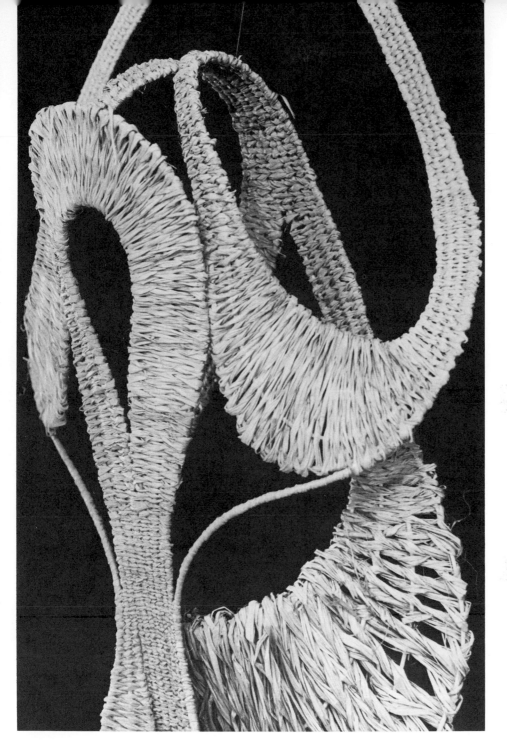

Opposite:
TROPHY and SKULL. Lillian Donald. TROPHY (*left*) is 53 inches high, 11 inches wide, 6 inches deep. Armatures of reeds are shaped and tacked on a wood surface to dry. The hardened armatures are filled in with raffia twined in different progressions and twists. Some wrapping. SKULL (*right*) is 26 inches high, 6 inches in diameter.
Above:
Detail of twining and structure of TROPHY armature.

Penobscot Indian Baskets. Contemporary. Braided sweet grass woven over colored brown ash strips.

Collection, Audrey Sylvester,
Durham, New Hampshire

6

Weaving

Weaving methods have long been an accepted technique for making baskets. Youngsters "weave" baskets of either paper or cane in primary grades and in Scout groups. And when the uninitiated person thinks of baskets it is immediately associated with "weaving." In past cultures very unsophisticated peoples produced extremely sophisticated woven baskets.

Weaving involves working with a single element, or one weft, over and under the warps. (It differs from twining, which is a two-element process; that is, two weft cords are worked simultaneously and they enclose the warp.) A multitude of weaving patterns appear in baskets, but the most prevalent is the simple Tabby or Plain Weave consisting of working one weft over one warp and under one warp. Shapes and variations possible with this plain weave are infinite. The Twill and Soumak patterns are also popular and these are illustrated with examples.

Weaving does not result in as solid a structure as does twining. Therefore, the woven basket is more often constructed of stiff materials such as willow, cane, and reed, and with grasses that provide a solid warp on which the woven materials can be built. Modern craftsmen tend to shy away from weaving when they wish to work solely with fibers. If they make a woven fiber piece, it may have to be stuffed with tissue, Dacron, or packing materials to retain its shape. Or it may have to be combined with twining and employ heavy cords that give the piece solidity and form.

All the problems and solutions for beginning, increasing, decreasing, and ending involved in twining apply to weaving. Usually the woven basket is begun from the base, though it can commence from the top and perhaps from a macramé Lark's Head and then be woven downward. It can be developed as a tubular weave with the shaping accomplished by increasing and decreasing warps.

Among the innovative contemporary woven baskets are the examples by Renie Adams and Gary Trentham. Prewoven strips of fabric have been fashioned into basketry forms. Also refer to page 125 for the tubular weave by Gary Trentham, which was stuffed and developed into a coiled basket.

Additions and decorative elements introduced earlier apply to woven baskets. Study baskets now on the market and those in museums to recognize the infinite forms and patterns, how they have been, and continue to be, used. Borrow motifs and details from woven baskets to apply to any of the forms you make in any technique or material.

BASIC WEAVING PROCEDURES

Basic weaving patterns that may be readily adapted to baskets worked in fibers and/or grasses include the following:

1. PLAIN WEAVE OR TABBY. The weft proceeds in a pattern of under one warp, over one warp. When the weft threads are beaten, or pushed, together, they form a compact pattern, as shown. To add a new length of weft, lay the new piece directly beneath the old one and weave them together for an inch or two. Then beat all the threads together, including the adjacent rows. Any loose ends can be worked in later with a crochet hook. Willows and hard weft materials may be laid on top of one another.

2. UNDER TWO, OVER TWO is a variation of plain weave. It is sometimes called "basket weave." You pass the weft under two warps, then over two warps. Alternate in the second row by going over the two warps you went under in the first row and under the next two. As you study the construction of baskets you will find this weave used extensively. Stripes are achieved by weaving two colors together or by alternating rows of color.

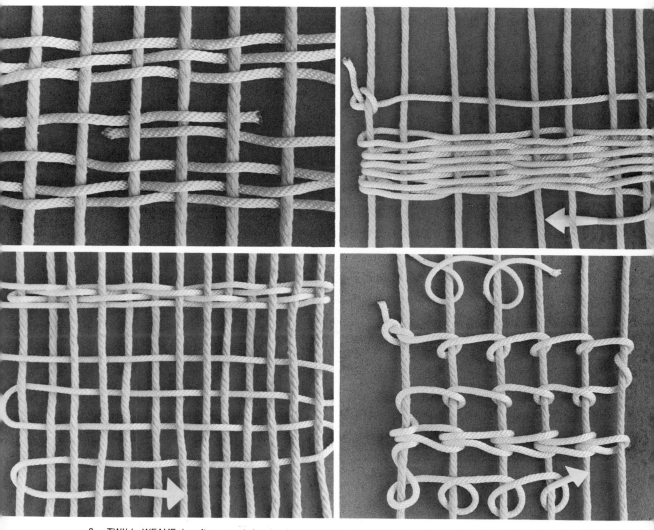

3. TWILL WEAVE is often used for basket bottoms and for progressive patterns on the sides. It yields a pattern of staggered diagonal wefts. The most often used twill weave is a variation of the over-two-under-two weave with each row staggered. Use an odd number of warps. For row 1, pass the weft over two, under two, with only one over at the end. For row 2, move the weft so it is staggered, as shown, and there are *two* cords *under* at the row's end. For row 3, stagger the weft over one more warp; end with one over and one under. To continue the diagonal twill, row 4 repeats row 1; row 5 repeats row 2; row 6 repeats row 3, etc. To reverse the twill for a herringbone, stagger the diagonal weft in the opposite direction.

4. The SOUMAK pattern involves "wrapping" each warp with a loop. The weft passes over the warp and loops behind it and over itself in front. Soumak, originally a rug-knotting method, appears in many fiber baskets and is frequently used in baskets from Indian and African cultures. It creates a raised pattern in contrast to plain weave or tabby. It is decorative and not used too often on utilitarian baskets because of the tendency for the ridges to wear out in time. When the knotted rows are separated, one appearance results; when they are pushed close together, the weave resembles the Stem Stitch in embroidery and also countered twining. Vary the appearance by working the loop over different warp combinations. Use stiff and soft yarns.

1. WOVEN WARP BASE. Any number of warps are crossed over and woven into one another. (Weave tightly; the loose weave is for demonstration only.) Then attach one or more weft strands and weave around the initial woven warps *but add in* one warp anywhere in the progression, because an uneven number of warps is necessary for weaving.

2. OVERLAID WARP BASE. Multiples of warps are placed over one another and bound together with a doubled weft that is twined around the first row or two. An additional warp is added to yield an uneven number of warps and the weaving progresses. Add new weft as shown in the PLAIN WEAVE photo, page 178.

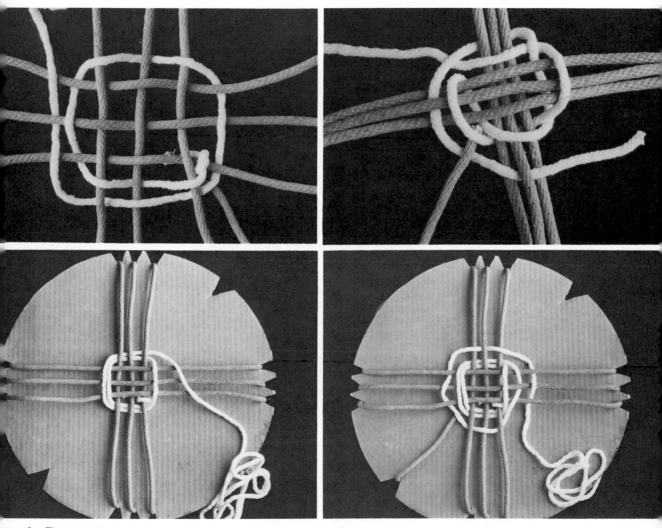

3. The woven base made out of traditional wood or cane is stiff and easy to weave around. When working with fibers, it helps to have the warps held taut as weaving progresses. A delicatessen cardboard from pizza is notched and serves as a loom device. The cords can be taped at the underside or carried around and then cut when the shaping begins.

4. Add in a warp, pinning it to the top, if necessary, and taping it at the back. Continue to weave the diameter of the bottom you require, adding in warps as necessary. When you are ready to begin shaping, remove the warp from the board and continue to weave on a foundation that is now relatively solid and easy to follow.

Traditional woven Chinese baskets frequently have the shapes of animals. Weaving can be manipulated into a variety of forms. The pattern is mainly a plain weave of over one, under one.

Collection, Ronald Jue, San Diego, California

Woven gold wire roosters. Mexico. The stiffness of wire is relatively easy to warp and is shaped as an armature for weaving using open and closed spaces.

Collection, Elvie Ten Hoor, Chicago, Illinois

TEA KETTLE WITH WATER. Helen Hennessey. 12 inches high, 14 inches wide. Woven and wrapped jute with stoneware beads. Hinged cover.

The bottom of a basket can begin with the warps overlapping. Marianne Rodwell. When the warp, or spokes, is covered, weaving can progress in many patterns and beads may be added. Much depends on the thickness and stiffness of the warp material.

Another way to begin the bottom of a woven basket. This one is stripped willow, but the same idea could be emulated in grouped fibers or a combination of grasses and fibers.

The base of an African basket, Upper Volta, is made from two layers of cane overlapped in opposing directions and the canes bent up to form the basket shape. A weaving pattern is evident on the bottom; the sides are held with a random weave. Two views.
Collection, Dona Meilach

A gold wire cup, Mexico. Observe how the warps are overlapped and spaced and then woven. The warps are brought up for the sides and woven at the top.
Collection, Elvie Ten Hoor,
Chicago, Illinois

EGG BASKET. Renie Adams. 4 inches high, 9-inch diameter. Card woven bands have been assembled over a crocheted base into a basket form. Woven ends are knotted. Eggs are crocheted.

BASKET WITH DARTS. Gary Trentham. 5 inches high, 11-inch diameter. Basket and dart forms were woven on a loom. The tubular woven darts were stuffed. The extra warp ends were knotted to make them stiff and the ends dipped in spray starch. The basket is made of black and white linen.

Headband. Cedar bark woven and wrapped has the shapes of two birds on top. This primitive piece could inspire other basketry forms and techniques in weaving and coiling.

Courtesy, Field Museum of Natural History, Chicago, Illinois

WILLOW BASKET. Lucy H. Traber. 30 inches high. Palm leaves woven in the Twill weave and combined with twining.
Courtesy, artist

FLAT BASKET. Lucy H. Traber. 26 inches high. New Zealand flax. A staggered over-two-under-two weave pattern is combined with a crossed-warp design on the sides of the basket.
Courtesy, artist

Woven fan. New Zealand. Palm.

Photo, Rubin Steinberg

Bamboo fan (detail). Japan. The grouped warps change weaving patterns as they expand outward.

Collection, Dona Meilach

ANIMAL MASK. Theo Ho. Weaving and fringe with appliqued features.

Courtesy, artist

Mask. Mexico. A woven facial form is enhanced with unplied hemp and wrapped strands at the top.

Collection, Dr. Earl Elman, Chicago, Illinois

WHITE LINEN. Gary Trentham. 7 inches high, 24-inch diameter. A completely Clove-Hitched basket has had fringed elements added between the hitching in each row in the same way elements are added to coiled forms.

7

Macramé

When macramé became popular late in the 1960s artists and craftsmen quickly adapted this ancient technique for making utilitarian objects and applied it to sculpture in an incredible variety of statements. True to their tradition, artists, now turning their thoughts to basketry, have realized that the macramé knots and resulting motifs are a perfect adjunct to coiling, twining, and weaving. In many examples, the entire basket form is knotted.

It is only proper, then, that macramé be introduced here as a basketry technique for it appears in more contemporary examples than the traditional weaving methods.

Macramé, which comes from the Arab word *migramah,* meaning "fringe," involves learning how to tie two basic knots: the Clove Hitch and the Square Knot. With these two knots, infinite shapes and motifs can be accomplished. Wed them with twining, crochet, or coiling and the versatility of all the techniques multiplies considerably.

We have already seen, in Chapter 5, how macramé can be used to begin and end a twined basket. But often a row or two of Clove Hitching, using a new weft cord with the existing warps, will result in a ridge or trim that cannot be achieved with twining alone. It is also possible to add warps onto this new weft so that a twined form can be expanded without the obvious addition that is indigenous to the twining method. This is demonstrated in Joan Sterrenburg's basket, page 210.

A basket composed completely of Clove Hitching holds its shape and is as sturdy as a coiled basket. Often, it is difficult to tell the difference between a coiled and a clove-hitched basket. Macramé baskets can be started from the top or bottom. Increasing is accomplished by adding new knotting cords over an anchor cord; decreasing, by simply omitting some of the knotting cords.

As you plan and form your baskets, think in terms of incorporating one technique with another to solve shape and design problems. Purism and tradition are blown to smithereens when a contemporary creative approach is sought.

If this is your first attempt at macramé, practice the knots on a foam working-board until they are easily done, and then attempt the basketry shapes. For additional macramé approaches refer to *Macramé: Creative Design in Knotting* by Dona Z. Meilach, also in the Crown Arts and Crafts Series.

Utilize wrapping methods and other embellishment ideas shown throughout the book.

UNTITLED. Kathryn McCardle. 22 inches high, 18 inches wide, 17 inches deep. Sisal. All Clove Hitching.

UNTITLED. Kathryn McCardle. Back view (*above*) and detail (*below*) of the basket on page 190. Clove Hitching results in a very sturdy, solid form when heavy cords are used.

THE CLOVE HITCH

The Clove Hitch is made by tying two loops over an anchor cord. The direction of the anchor cord determines the angle of the Clove Hitch bar—horizontal or diagonal. It may also be tied vertically. It can be tied around a circular form and therefore is ideal for basketry. The working cord (weft) is mounted over the anchor cord (this acts as the core, or warp, in coiling). It can begin with a Lark's Head knot (shown below), a Picot, or a Clove Hitch. For the Lark's Head, double the working cord and place it under the anchor cord. Reach through the resulting loop and pull the ends through; these ends become your working cords.

HORIZONTAL CLOVE HITCH LEFT TO RIGHT

1.   This involves tying two loops around an anchor cord.
a. Pin the left strand of the first cord as shown and place it horizontally over all the vertical cords.
b. Bring the knotting strand from under the anchor, loop it over and around to the left and through the loop, as shown. This is the first half of the Clove Hitch. Tighten the loop.
c. The second half of the knot is made to the right of the first loop. It begins over the anchor cord, loops around to the left and through, as shown.

2.   Continue to tie each strand individually around the anchor cord using the two loops of the Clove Hitch. As each loop is tied, push it next to the previous loop to achieve an even appearance. Tie a small knot in the end of the anchor cord to identify it and avoid confusing it with the knotting strands.

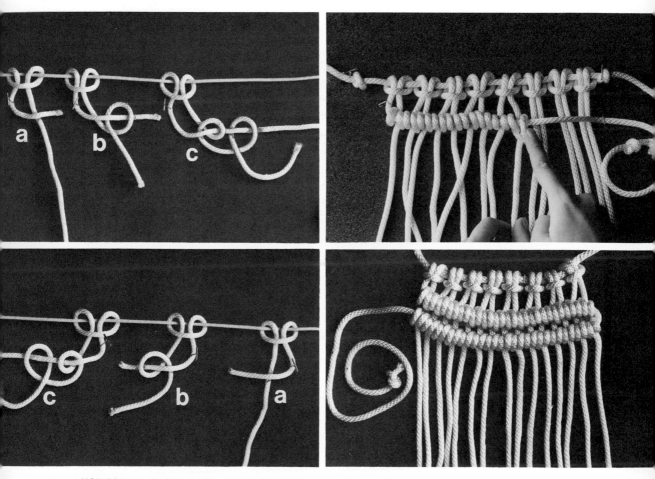

HORIZONTAL CLOVE HITCH RIGHT TO LEFT

3.   To create a second bar, the Clove Hitch is worked in reverse from right to left, using the same anchor cord pinned or held taut across all the strands.
a. Hold or pin the anchor cord taut over the knotting strands. Begin knotting with first strand on the right next to the anchor cord.
b. Loop the knotting strand from under the anchor around, over, and through, as shown. Tighten.
c. Bring knotting strand over the anchor cord and to the left of the first half of the knot for the second loop, working it around and through, as shown. Continue to tie each strand individually around the anchor to complete a bar knotted from right to left.

4.   The finished two horizontal bars will appear like this. You will discover that the cord used for the anchor shortens more rapidly than the knotting cords. With experience, you will learn to plan for anchor cords and make them two to three times longer than the knotting cords.

VERTICAL CLOVE HITCH

The Clove Hitch may be tied vertically. For Vertical Hitches in basketry a new length of cord is usually introduced and clove-hitched over the vertical cords. This one knotting cord is used up quickly, so always make it very long. Vertical Hitching can precede or follow twined and woven sections of baskets.

LEFT TO RIGHT

1a. Pin or tie the knotting cord into the work. Bring the knotting cord *under* the first vertical warp on the left.
b. Loop the weft *over* the warp to the front, then around and through for the first half of the knot.
c. The second half of the knot is looped *over* the warp and around, as shown.

2. Continue the Vertical Clove Hitch by placing the weft *under* each warp and Clove Hitching with the same cord each knot.

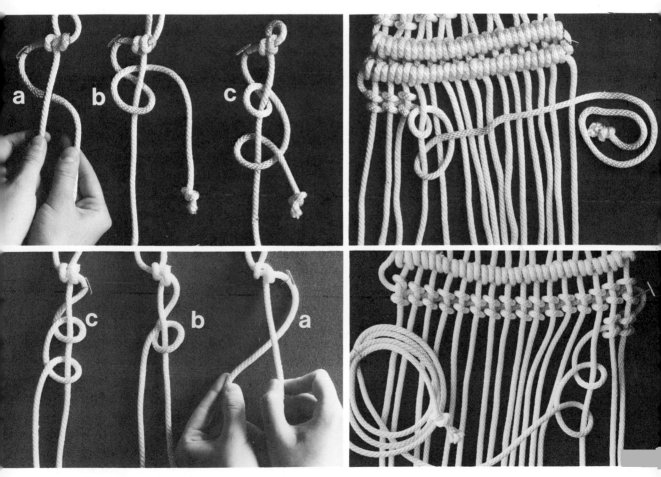

RIGHT TO LEFT

3. This involves exactly the opposite procedure of the left-to-right knot.
a. Pin or tie the weft around one warp and bring the weft, or knotting cord, *under* the vertical warp.
b. Loop the weft to the right *over* the warp, around and through at the top of the loop.
c. Make the second half of the Hitch *over* the warp to the right, around the top of the loop, and through. Continue by bringing the weft under each strand and repeating the directions until as many rows as necessary are complete.

4. When one cord is used for knotting it shortens very rapidly. For each row of Vertical Clove Hitching, use a cord approximately three times the circumference of the basket. Clove Hitching provides an easy method for alternating colors of one or more rows for a horizontally striped pattern. Any loose ends can be worked into the basket and later poked under the knotting and glued or stitched to secure them. If added strands will be introduced, long loose ends may be left on the outside of the basket to work into the design.

1.   You can use the Clove Hitch in a circular manner by beginning from the bottom of a basket and increasing when you want to expand the shape. To narrow the circumference of the basket, omit or decrease working cords.

Pin a circle to a working board and mount as many working cords as you wish with a Lark's Head. Make the beginning circular cord long and continue to use this as your anchor cord. Tie Clove Hitches around the anchor cord, knotting each strand of the working cord *over* the anchor cord. To increase, fold new working cords over the anchor and work them in. If you want the shape to be symmetrical, add in even numbers of cords around the shape in the same row. For odd shapes, add in cords wherever and whenever necessary for the form you envision.

2.   You can also begin knotting a basket from the top with the plain Lark's Head or with a decorative Picot beginning. It helps to work over a shape about the size of the basket you wish to make until the form begins to grow and become stiff. Work over a ball, a bowl, a cone, piece of Styrofoam, a pillow—anything that you can improvise to begin.

PICOT

SINGLE LOOP PICOT
The simplest way to begin a Picot is shown finished (*at left*) and the procedure (*right*). Mount each cord to be used onto a holding line. Tie the first strand with a Clove Hitch, then pin a loop at the desired height above the holding line to the knotting board and tie the second strand with a Clove Hitch. The result will be a series of loops above the holding line. This is the principle of Picots regardless of how complex the knots are in the loop above the line.

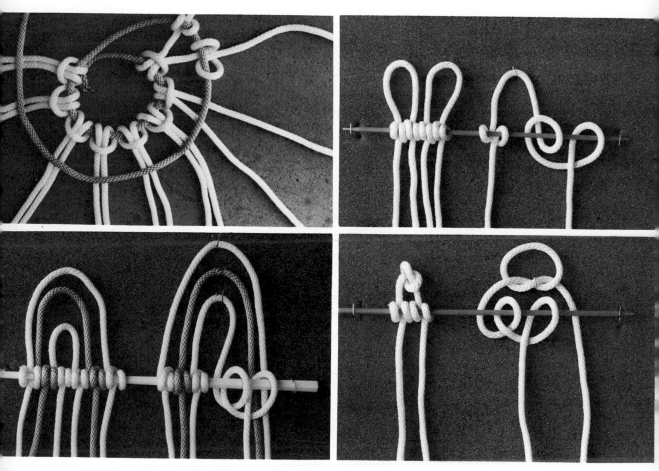

MULTIPLE LOOP PICOT

3.   A series of loops in varying sizes makes an attractive border. Use one or more cords. Pin the three loops to the board as shown. Place a holding line over the strands and Clove Hitch them.

OVERHAND KNOT PICOT

4.   A more decorative Picot can be made by tying an Overhand Knot in the loop before Clove Hitching the second strand.

SQUARE KNOTTING

The Square Knot can be used as a motif within a basket, between Clove Hitches, and wherever you might want to improvise. It can be used to begin a basket from the top. By alternating the Square Knot strands in different progressions an entire basket could be made, but, unless the knots were tied closely together, the form would not be stiff enough to be self-supporting in most fibers. It is successful for hanging baskets.

The Square Knot is usually tied with multiples of four cords. The inside cords serve as anchor cords for the two outside knotting cords.

a. Begin with four cords. Bring the *right* cord *over* and to the *left* of the two anchor cords.
b. Place the *left* cord over the *right* cord.
c. Bring the left cord *under* the anchors and up through the loop formed by the right cord.
d. Pull, and you have the first half of the Square Knot.

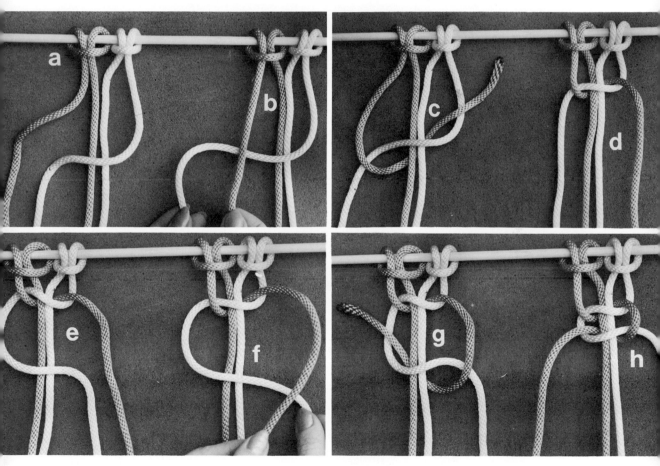

e. For the second half of the knot, bring the *left* cord over and to the *right* of the two anchor cords and place the *right* cord over it.
f. Bring the right cord *under* the anchors and up through the loop formed by the left cord.
g. Pull the cords . . .
h. The finished knot.

A conical basketlike shape evolves quickly with Clove Hitching and Square Knotting. The form was begun from a circular cord pinned to a cardboard cone from weaving yarn and then worked downward.

Knotted basket shapes in progress. At center back, the beginning is a looped Picot.

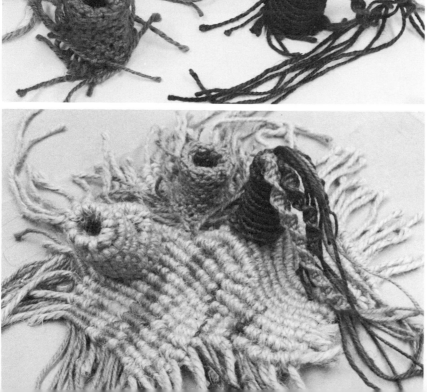

Basketry knotted forms attached to a Clove-Hitched base that undulates and gives the feeling of mountains on a landscape. Felicia Smith.

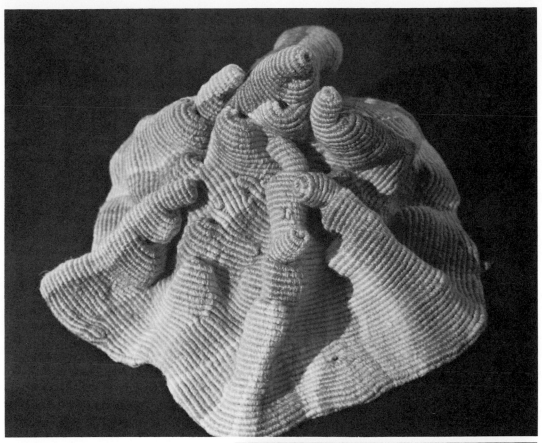

FREE FORM. Diane Itter. 5 inches high, 9-inch diameter. Clove Hitching can be worked in any direction, depending on the angle of the anchor cord. Below, work in progress.

Four views of a free-form basket. Diane Sheehan. 7 inches high, 10-inch diameter. Cotton and raffia; all Clove Hitching. The bottom of the basket uses the back of the knot. In some of the open spaces, the cords are twisted for added strength.

FUNGI. Eileen Bernard. Several takeoffs on basket shapes have been combined in this funky sculptural form composed mainly of Clove Hitching and some wrapping. Square Knots are added at borders. The center is a wrapped wood stick.

Photo, Lee Snadow

>

BASKET FORM. Gayle Luchessa. A Siamese-twin-like basket shape utilizes tightly worked Clove Hitching for the basket and a more open shaping at the top. Portions of the Clove Hitching are folded back to expose and utilize the texture and design of the back of the knot.

Courtesy, artist

KNOTTED BASKET. Ferne Jacobs. 6 inches high, 7-inch diameter. Rayon, straw, linen, and metallic threads.
Courtesy, artist

UNTITLED. Kathryn McCardle. 15 inches high, 11-inch diameter. Knotting with linen and handspun wool. Some of the knotting "cords" are strips of handwoven wool.

Top:
STANDING CYLINDERS. Suellen Glashausser. Green and yellow lawn-chair webbing is Clove-Hitched. The weather-resistant material is perfect for outdoor sculptures.

Courtesy, artist

Bottom:
Detail of lawn chair webbing, Clove-Hitched.

>

UNTITLED. Gayle Luchessa. 15 inches high, 12 inches wide. Clove Hitching that grew from a basket shape into a sculpture.

Courtesy, artist

UNTITLED. Ferne Jacobs. 6 inches high, 6-inch diameter. Knotted basket with fringed endings.

Courtesy, artist

MY PRE-COLUMBIAN WATER JUG. Gervaise Livingston. 19 inches high, 41-inch diameter. Knotted and twined to simulate basket techniques in natural linen and black mohair. Motifs are taken from a Pre-Columbian vase.

Photo, Morton Witz

UNTITLED. Gary Trentham. 10 inches high, 10-inch diameter. Red linen. Intricate Clove Hitching.
Collection, Joan Sterrenburg, Bloomington, Indiana

UNTITLED. Renie Adams. Crocheted bottom and tightly Clove-Hitched sides with colored rayon threads added.

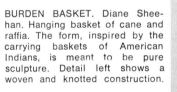

BURDEN BASKET. Diane Sheehan. Hanging basket of cane and
raffia. The form, inspired by the
carrying baskets of American
Indians, is meant to be pure
sculpture. Detail left shows a
woven and knotted construction.

209

BASKET. Joan Sterrenburg. 13 inches high, 16-inch diameter. A combination of twining and Clove Hitching enables the basketmaker to expand a form without adding cords obtrusively. Varying the types and color of cords used adds design and texture.

Detail of above.

BASKET. Diane Itter. 6½ inches high, 11-inch diameter. Linen and cotton Clove-Hitched. Added colors also were functional as cords to increase the shape.

Detail of above. The top was started with the Picot mounting.

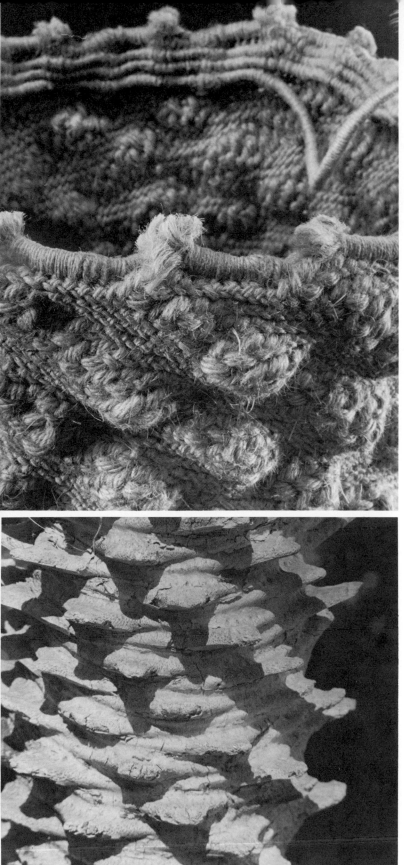

Opposite page:
BASKET. Joan Sterren-
burg. 14 inches high, 16-
inch diameter. Wartlike appearance resulted from
knotting two kinds of cord
with different thicknesses
and pulling them tightly;
heavy jute and thin linen.
The form was begun at the
bottom and expanded.

It is interesting that the
detail has an appearance
similar to the bark of a
palm tree (*below*). Mrs.
Sterrenburg did not emu-
late the tree, but could
have. This shows how
much art borrows from na-
ture, which is always a
source for design con-
cepts.

Basket forms that utilize the Clove Hitch and Buttonhole Stitch are freely developed by Rubin Steinberg. Many of the ending techniques he uses are based on a study of Maori weaving, and he shares some of these motifs in the following demonstrations. He uses heavy, different-textured ropes and works them through with a pliers. Ends of weft cords are tightly bound with adhesive tape to form a sharp, needlelike working point.

1. Tools used are needle-nose pliers and straight pliers, scissors, adhesive tape, awls, masking tape, glue, pins, and wire brushes. The brushes may be used to bring up a texture in parts of the work.

2. Mr. Steinberg's method for beginning a basket form is entirely his own. He begins by making a Lark's Head with one cord over a group of knotting cords.

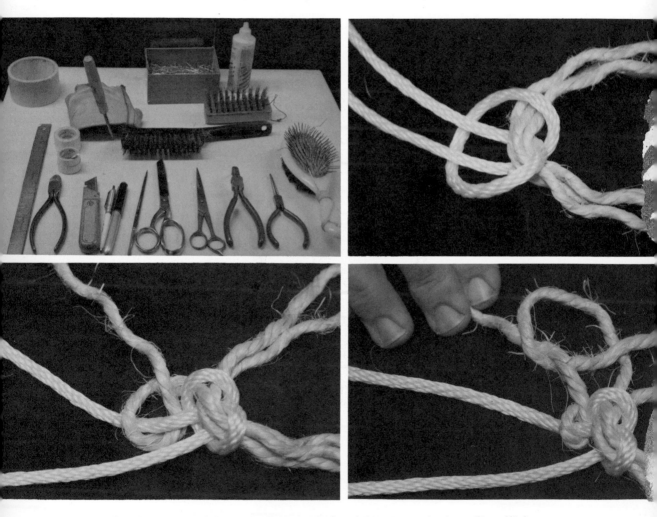

3. Each knotting strand, in turn, is tied over one leg of the warp cord using a Clove Hitch.

4. Then, a second weft strand is knotted over a first weft strand . . .

5.   . . . and brought over a warp.

6.   The knotting builds up in this manner and provides a tightly knotted base on which to build any shape.

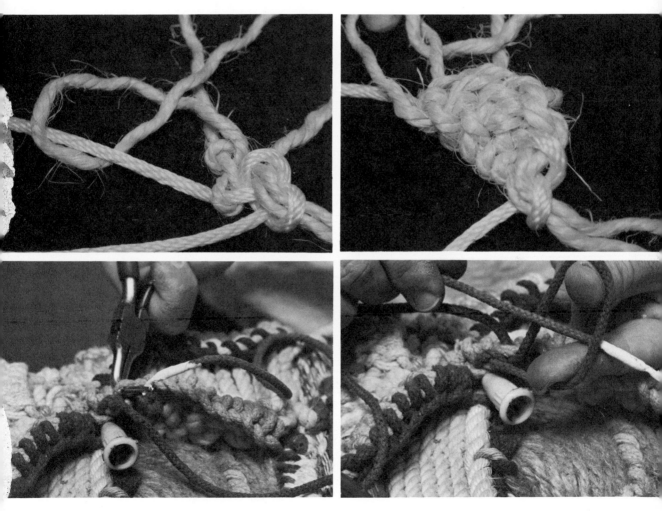

7.   The working (weft) cord is pulled through a ridge formed by the preceding knots.

8.   The taped, pointed weft cord is brought through the loop to make a Buttonhole Stitch.

BASKET FORM. Rubin Steinberg. Approximately 22 inches high, 18 inches wide.

1. Details from Rubin Steinberg's basket forms: A fringed area may be in the middle or any portion of the work as well as at the top. The end is held taut by introducing a new weft cord and Vertical Clove Hitching over each ending cord.

2. An exposed core may be allowed to protrude for motif and design element.

3. The knotting can be shaped by pulling some areas very tight.

4. Braiding can be used for endings.

1. An edge partially knotted . . .

2. . . . is completed by tying a Vertical Clove Hitch with a new cord over each knotting cord.

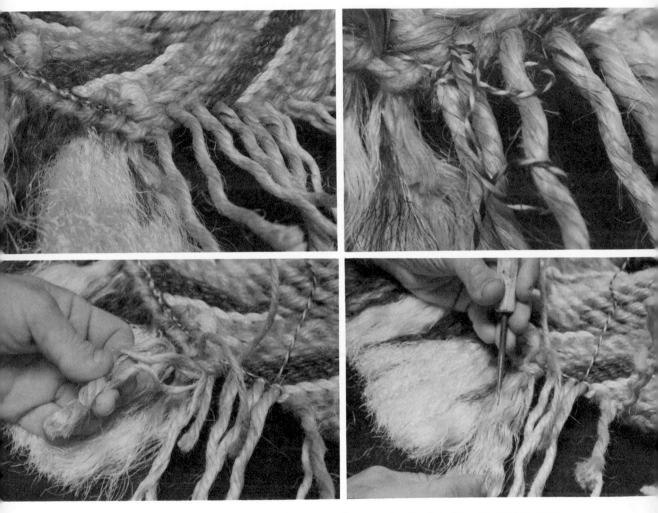

3. To achieve unplied endings; untwist the rope in the opposite direction from the original twist.

4. Then smooth out the plies with the point of an awl; later it can be brushed with a wire brush.

Two mask forms by Rubin Steinberg show the versatility of his knotting method. Both begin from a base of a few knots (shown on pages 214 and 215), and then the knotting expands outward. There are no traditional coils as used in basketry, or anchor cords as used in macramé.

HANGING. Rubin Steinberg. 20 inches high, 36 inches wide. Clove Hitching and basketry-ending methods are applied to a wall hanging.

8

Crochet

Crochet is strictly a contemporary approach to basketry. It does not appear in traditional basketry books. But examples of crocheted forms resulting from the new interest in basketry are numerous and innovative. Crochet, then, becomes another basketry technique when used in the basketmaker's context.

Crochet is accomplished with a hook that creates loops made within one another. Crochet can be developed in flat, cylindrical, or free-form shapes. It usually requires soft yarns that have some "stretch" to them. The resulting forms are not so solid and self-supporting as those made from nonstretchy yarns and by coiling, twining, or knotting. Even if jute or nonstretchy threads are crocheted, the form will not necessarily retain the shape desired. Therefore, a crocheted basket may have to be stuffed with cotton, Dacron, tissue, or the like, or it can be worked over an armature of wire or other solid material.

The most important approach to the crocheted basket is to think in terms of assembling one or more parts. Shaping can be accomplished by increasing and decreasing, but often these produce gradual, rather than sharp, bold turns and edges. It is often more expedient to make a base separately, then attach the cylindrical sides.

For more solidity, crocheted parts are easily combined with coiled, twined, or woven portions, and examples of this are illustrated.

Projecting parts can be added elements, although crochet allows you to work a chain out from solid portions and bring it back again. You can pick up loops and crochet entire new portions onto them.

Lori Kratovil, whose many crocheted baskets appear in this chapter, believes that learning to crochet for artistic purposes gives you much more freedom than if you have already crocheted from patterns for sweaters, hats, and so forth. You don't have prelearned ideas of how to go about forming a shape; you simply use the hook and thread and let it work at will. You can poke in and pull out sections and fool around with them until you are satisfied with the shape. Or you can leave this prerogative to the viewer because you may want him or her to experience, in a small way, how a basket is shaped. Once you learn the simple-to-do crochet procedures, you can readily form baskets and anything else within the realm of this needlework art.

<

SPHERE FIVE. Susan H. Brown. Crocheted basket forms with feathers. Some are made with removable lids.

Courtesy, artist

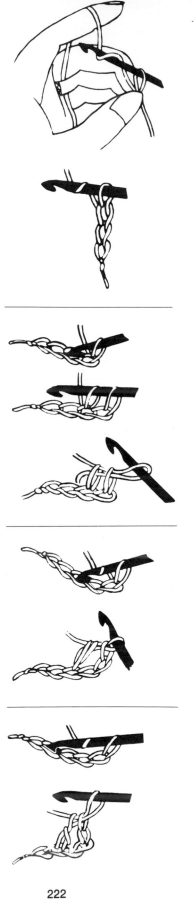

CROCHET

All crochet begins with a simple chain accomplished with a plastic, wood, or metal crochet hook. Large crochet loops can be made using your fingers as the hook, and this is often referred to as "finger crochet."

CROCHET CHAIN

1. Place a slipknot on hook held with the point toward you, as you would hold a pencil. Hold yarn in the other hand over your ring finger, under middle and over index finger, loosely enough so the yarn feeds smoothly as the hook pulls it.

2. Pass hook under and over yarn and draw it through the loop on the hook for as many stitches as you want the chain to be.

SINGLE CROCHET

1. Insert hook under two top strands of second stitch from hook. *For all crochet, hook is always inserted under both top loops* unless a different motif is desired.

2. Pass hook under and over yarn and draw it through the stitch to give you two loops on the hook.

3. Pass hook under and over yarn again and draw it through the two loops.

HALF DOUBLE CROCHET

1. Pass hook under and over yarn, insert hook into third stitch from hook.

2. Pass hook under and over yarn and draw it through stitch. Pass hook under and over yarn again and draw it through the three loops on the hook.

DOUBLE CROCHET

1. Pass hook under and over yarn, insert hook into the fourth stitch from hook.

2. Pass hook under and over yarn and draw it through the stitch. Pass hook under and over yarn again. Draw yarn through the first two loops only on the hook. Pass hook under and over yarn again and draw it through the remaining two loops on hook.

TRIPLE CROCHET

1. Pass hook under and over yarn twice. Insert hook into the fifth stitch from hook.

2. Pass hook under and over yarn and draw it through the stitch. *Pass hook under and over yarn and draw through two loops, repeat from * twice.

INCREASING

Increasing is simple. You work two of whatever stitch you are doing anywhere in the row or at the end. Increasing is usually done with a single or double crochet.

DECREASING

Decrease can be made at any point and is usually done in a single or double crochet; each one is slightly different.

To Decrease in Single Crochet

1. Insert hook in stitch next to loop and draw yarn through (two loops on hook), insert hook in next stitch and draw yarn through (three loops on hook).

2. Pass hook under and over yarn and draw through all three loops. You actually work two stitches together to give a decrease of one.

To Decrease in Double Crochet

1. Pass hook under and over yarn, insert hook in next stitch and drawn yarn through. There are three loops on hook.

2. Pass hook under and over and draw through two loops with two remaining on hook. Hook under and over yarn again.

3. Insert hook in next stitch and draw yarn through; four loops on hook.

4. Catch yarn again and draw through two loops; three loops remain on hook.

5. Catch yarn and draw through the three loops. A decrease of one double crochet is completed.

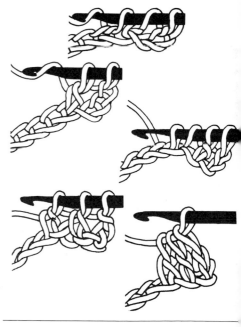

To Form a Circle

1. Make a chain of any number of stitches. Insert hook in first chain made. Catch yarn with hook. Be sure chain is not twisted.

2. Draw yarn through *both* the chain and the loop on hook. This is a "slip stitch," which can be used for any kind of joining. You now have a circle that can be expanded to any size you like using the same number of stitches to form a straight tubular crochet; or it can be shaped by increasing and decreasing.

THE GREAT MOTHER. Gayle Luchessa. 8 feet high, 5 feet wide. Jute and wool. Crochet, knotless netting or looping, and some weaving and coiling. The same techniques applied to basketry can be applied to wall forms.

Photo, Marion Ferri

TORSO BASKET. Mary Lou Higgins. 8 inches high, 22 inches wide, 13 inches deep. The container area is shaped of aluminum wire; gray-green wool and linen are crocheted onto the wire form. The arms and hands are wool and linen stuffed with polyester fill.

Photo, Edward Higgins

JEWEL BOX. Renie Adams. 3½ inches high, 3-inch diameter. Beads, 30 inches long. Crocheted jewel box with cover. Crocheted white beads have a gold crocheted clasp.

CUP AND SAUCER. Renie Adams. Saucer, 5-inch diameter. Cup, 2½ inches high, 2¾-inch diameter at top. Crochet with imbrication. The extra colored threads are added as the work progresses. Note that no color appears inside the cup although the outside is as colorfully decorated as the saucer. They form a matching set.

STILL LIFE OF A STILL LIFE (detail). Renie Adams. 2¾ inches high, 5½ inches wide, 2¼ inches deep. Crochet with imbrication.

POT AND CUPS WITH THEIR OWN SHADOWS. Renie Adams. 2¼ inches high, 8 inches wide, 7-inch diameter. Crochet and embroidery. The actual shadow that would fall from side lighting has been incorporated onto the base.

ARBOL VIEJO. Lori Kratovil. 14 inches high, 9-inch diameter. Yarn and brown polished cord. Crochet and macramé. The form is stuffed. Crocheting was started at the top and increased and expanded, then macramé added for the base.

A BOX FOR SOMETHING SPECIAL. Teri Holdcraft. 8 inches high, 3½-inch bottom diameter. Variegated cotton, rayon, and wool. Crochet and Clove Hitching.

WOMB TOMB. Lori Kratovil. 11½ inches high, 8½-inch diameter. Crochet top joined to macramé base. Top and bottom are joined with Square Knotting. Some embroidery added over the Clove-Hitched base.

POLYP. Lori Kratovil. 13½ inches high, 12-inch diameter. Yarn and brown polished cord. The base is stuffed. Top and base are developed separately, then combined. Macramé is added in and the excess cord allowed to dangle. See detail (*right*) of back and underneath side where base and top are attached and macramé worked in.

BASKET HANGING. Esther Gotthoeffer. 42 inches high, 28 inches wide in this arrangement. Crocheted jute. Basketry concepts inspired this changeable hanging that can be rearranged in multiple relationships of one part to another.

RED CONVERTIBLE. Lori Kratovil. 11 inches high, 6½-inch diameter. Crocheted yarn. The form was begun and the top developed into a free-moving shape that can be arranged according to the viewer's whims. The soft basket shape has, of course, become sculptural.

GREEN BEAN. Lori Kratovil. 12½ inches high, 12-inch diameter. Crocheted yarn, begun at the top. Appendages and negative spaces can be developed as the crochet progresses, or parts can be added later. The crochet technique is extremely versatile for basketry.

LAMP. Mary Lou Higgins. 54 inches high, 20 inches wide, 15 inches deep. Crocheted basket forms result in a lamp crocheted over a wire structure. Acrilan fiber and beads and turkey and pheasant feathers.

Photo, Edward K. Higgins

LAMP. Mary Lou Higgins. 50 inches high, 20 inches wide, 20 inches deep. Wire armature. Acrilan fibers, lynx fur, beads, and turkey and pheasant feathers.

Photo, Edward K. Higgins

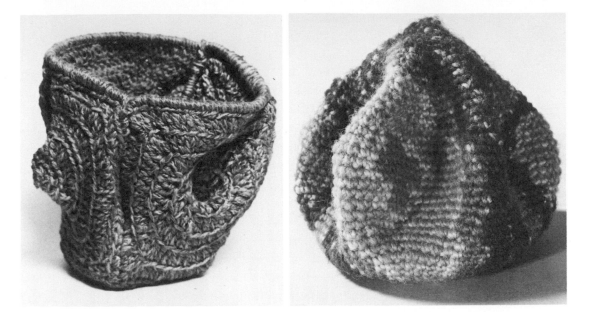

RED CONTAINER. Mary Lou Higgins. 6½ inches high, 6 inches wide, 5 inches deep. Crocheted mixed red fibers on a free-form aluminum wire shape. Crochet was worked into the wire and then additional crochet worked onto itself to expand the form.

Photo, Edward K. Higgins

CLOSED CONTAINER. Judith I. Kleinberg. 3½ inches high. Single-ply wool which has been ikat dyed to create color patterns as it was crocheted.

Photo, Royal A. Lyons

CERAMIC AND FIBER CONSTRUCTION #2. Judith I. Kleinberg. 5½ inches high, 9-inch diameter. Crocheted wool and silk with glazed stoneware. Densely crocheted fabric assumes a surprisingly solid and heavy form that maintains its shape without stuffing.

Photo, Royal A. Lyons

VASE. Pamela Stearn. 15 inches high. Multicolored cotton and wool yarns. The combination of crochet and knotting with different yarns results in a bumpy surface and a rich texture.

Photographed at the Richmond
Art Center, Richmond, California

For Your Information

The following books and pamphlets may be consulted for further information on the history of basketry and for contemporary allied techniques and ideas for design.

I. BASKETRY

Allen, Elsie. *Pomo Basketmaking.* Healdsburg, California: Naturegraph Publishers, 1972.

Blanchard, Mary Mills. *The Basketry Book.* New York: Charles Scribner's Sons, 1914.

Bobart, H. H. *Basketwork Through the Ages.* England: Oxford University Press, 1936.

Brigham, William Tufts. *Mat and Basket Weaving of the Ancient Hawaiians.* Honolulu: Bishop Museum Press, 1906.

Christopher, Frederick John. *Basketry.* New York: Dover Publications, Inc., 1952.

Cooke, Viva, and Sampley, Julia. *Palmetto Braiding and Weaving.* Peoria, Illinois: The Manual Arts Press, 1947.

Crowfoot, Grace M. *Textiles, Basketry and Mats.* A History of Technology, 1954 (Cumulative Publication).

"Basketry," *Encyclopaedia Britannica,* vol. 3. Chicago: The University of Chicago, 1972.

Fitzgerald, Sallie G. *Lessons in Reed Weaving.* Boston: The Priscilla Publishing Co., 1924.

Florance, Norah. *Rush-Work.* London: G. Bell & Sons, Ltd., 1962. (Distributed by Sportshelf, New Rochelle, New York.)

Gallinger, Osma (Palmer) Couch. *Basket Pioneering.* New York: Orange Judd Publishing Co., 1933. (Rev. edition, New York: Orange Judd Publishing Co., 1940.)

Goodloe, William H., *Coconut Palm Frond Weaving.* Rutland, Vt.: Charles E. Tuttle Co., Inc., 1972.

Harvey, Marian. *Crafts of Mexico.* New York: Macmillan Publishing Co., 1973.

Heizer and Whipple. *The California Indians* (a source book). Berkeley, California: University of California Press, 1962.

Hosking, Phyllis. *Basket-Making for Amateurs.* London: G. Bell & Sons, Ltd., 1960.

James, George Wharton. *Indian Basketry.* Henry Malkan, 1909. (Facsimile edition, New York: Dover Publications, Inc., 1972.)

————. *Indian Basketry and How To Make Indian and Other Baskets.* New York: Henry Malkan, 1903. (Facsimile edition, Glorieta, New Mexico: Rio Grande Press, 1970.)

————. *Practical Basket Making.* Cambridge, Mass., and Newark, New Jersey: J. L. Hammett Publications, 1951. (Facsimile edition, Shorey Publishers.)

Kissell, Mary L. *Basketry of the Papago and Pima Indians.* Anthropological Papers of the American Museum of Natural History, vol. 17, pt. 4. Glorieta, New Mexico: Rio Grande Press, 1972.

Klipfel, Werner. *Basket Weaving.* West Germany: Herder, 1968.

Krouche, Greta. *Weaving with Cane and Reed—Modern Basketry.* New York: Van Nostrand Reinhold Co., 1968.

Lamb, Dr. Frank W. *Indian Baskets of North America.* Riverside, California: Riverside Museum Press, 1972.

Lammer, Jutta. *Make Things with Straw and Raffia.* New York: Watson-Guptill, 1965.

Lang, Mrs. Edwin. *Basketry, Weaving and Design.* New York: Charles Scribner's Sons, 1926.

Lang, Mrs. Minnie McAfee. *Reed Weaving.* New York: Charles Scribner's Sons, 1925.

Lyford, Carrie A. *Iroquois Crafts.* Lawrence, Kansas: United States Department of Interior, Bureau of Indian Affairs, 1945.

Mason, Otis Tufton. "Aboriginal American Basketry." *Report of the United States National Museum,* 1902. (Facsimile edition, Glorieta, New Mexico: Rio Grande Press, 1970.)

————. "Vocabulary of Malaysian Basket-work." A Study in the W. L. Abbott Collection, No. 1631. *Proceedings of the United States National Museum.* Washington, D.C.: Government Printing Office, 1909.

Navajo School of Indian Basketry. *Indian Basket Weaving.* 1903. (Facsimile edition, New York: Dover Publications, Inc., 1971.)

Paul, Frances. *Spruce Root Basketry of the Alaska Tlingit.* Lawrence, Kansas: United States Department of the Interior, Bureau of Indian Affairs, 1944.

Roberts, Helen H. *Basketry of the San Carlos Apache Indians.* Anthropological Papers of the American Museum of Natural History, vol. 31, pt. 2. Glorieta, New Mexico: Rio Grande Press, 1972.

Robinson, A. Lambert E. *Basket Weaver of Arizona.* Albuquerque, New Mexico: University of New Mexico Press, 1954.

Rossbach, Ed. *Baskets as Textile Art.* New York: Van Nostrand Reinhold Co., 1973.

Sandford, Lettice, and Davis, Philla. *Decorative Straw Work and Corn Dollies.* London: B. T. Batsford, Ltd., 1964.

Tinsley, Laura Rollins. *Practical and Artistic Basketry.* New York: A. S. Barnes Co., 1904.

Whiteford, Andrew Hunter. *North American Indian Arts.* New York: Golden Press, 1970.

Wright, Dorothy. *The Complete Guide to Basket Weaving.* New York: Drake Publishers, Inc., 1972.

II. WEAVING, TWINING

Atwater, Mary Meigs. *Byways in Handweaving.* New York: Macmillan Co., 1954.

Collingwood, Peter. *The Techniques of Rug Weaving.* New York: Watson-Guptill, 1968.

D'Harnoncourt, René, et al., eds. *Textiles of Ancient Peru and Their Techniques.* Seattle, Washington: The University of Washington Press, 1962.

Emery, Irene. *The Primary Structures of Fabrics.* Washington, D.C.: The Textile Museum, 1966.

Eppendorff, Lina. *Handwork Construction.* Brooklyn, New York: Published by the author, 1908.

Hartung, Rolf. *Creative Textile Design: Thread and Fabric.* New York. Van Nostrand Reinhold Co., 1964.

Harvey, Virginia, and Tidball, Harriet. *Weft Twining.* California: Craft and Hobby Book Service, 1969.

Hopa, Ngapare. *The Art of Piupiu Making.* Sydney: A. H. & A. W. Reed, 1971.

Johnson, William H., and Newkirk, Louis V. *The Textile Arts.* New York: Macmillan Co., 1944.

Mead, Sidney M. *The Art of Taaniko Weaving.* Sydney: A. H. & A. W. Reed, 1968.

Meilach, Dona Z., and Snow, Lee Erlin. *Weaving Off-Loom.* Chicago: Henry Regnery Publishing Co., 1973.

Nordland, Odd. *Primitive Scandinavian Textiles in Knotless Netting.* Norway: Oslo University Press, 1961.

Rainey, Sarita R. *Weaving Without a Loom.* Worcester, Massachusetts: Davis Publications, 1969.

Regensteiner, Elsa. *The Art of Weaving.* New York: Van Nostrand Reinhold Co., 1970.

Turner, Alta R. *Finger Weaving: Indian Braiding.* New York: Sterling Publishing Co., Inc., 1973.

Wilson, Jean. *Weaving Is for Anyone.* New York: Van Nostrand Reinhold Co., 1967.

III. MACRAMÉ

Ashley, Clifford W. *The Ashley Book of Knots.* New York: Doubleday & Co., Inc., 1944.

Bress, Helene. *The Macramé Book.* New York: Charles Scribner's Sons, 1972.

de Dillmont, Thérèse. *Encyclopedia of Needlework.* Mulhouse, France. (Facsimile edition, Philadelphia: Running Press, Inc., 1972.)

Harvey, Virginia. *Color and Design in Macramé.* New York: Van Nostrand Reinhold Co., 1972.

Meilach, Dona Z. *Macramé Accessories.* New York: Crown Publishers, 1972.

―――. *Macramé, Creative Design in Knotting.* New York: Crown Publishers, 1971.

Paque, Joan Michaels. *Design Principles and Fiber Techniques.* Shorewood, Wisconsin: Published by the author, 1973.

―――. *Visual Instructional Macramé.* Shorewood, Wisconsin: Published by the author, 1972.

IV. DYES

Lesch, Alma. *Vegetable Dyeing.* New York: Watson-Guptill Publishing Co., 1970.

Meilach, Dona Z. *Contemporary Batik and Tie-dye.* New York: Crown Publishers, 1973.

Schetky, Ethel Jane, and staff, eds. *Dye Plants and Dyeing—A Handbook,* Brooklyn, New York: Brooklyn Botanic Garden, 1964.

V. INSPIRATION AND DESIGN SOURCES

Austin, Robert, and Ueda, Koichiro. *Bamboo.* New York & Tokyo: A Weatherhill Book, 1970.

Bain, George. *The Methods of Construction of Celtic Art.* Glasgow: William MacClellan Publishers, 1951.

Boas, Franz. *Primitive Art.* New York: Dover Publications, Inc., 1955.

Constantine, Mildred, and Larsen, Jack Lenor. *Beyond Craft: The Art Fabric.* New York: Van Nostrand Reinhold, 1973.

Hiroa, Te Rangi (Peter H. Buck). *Arts and Crafts of Hawaii.* Bernice P. Bishop Museum Special Publication 45, 1962.

Meilach, Dona Z. *Creating Art from Fibers and Fabrics.* Chicago: Henry Regnery Publishing Co., 1972.

Oka, Hideyuki. *How to Wrap Five Eggs. Japanese Design in Traditional Packaging.* New York: Harper and Row Publishers, 1965.

Otsuka, Sueko. *Fancy Ribbon Tying.* Japan Publications, 1964.

Petrie, Flinders. *Decorative Patterns of the Ancient World.* London, 1930.

Sieber, Roy. *African Textiles and Decorative Arts.* New York: The Museum of Modern Art, 1972.

Trowell, Margaret. *African Design.* London: Faber and Faber, Ltd., 1960.

VI. PAMPHLETS

Basketry. New York: Alnap Co., Inc., 66 Reade Street, N.Y. 10007.

Basketry. Walnut Creek, California: Civic Arts Gallery (Catalog of exhibition), 1973.

Cane and Raffia. New York: Herder and Herder, 1969.

Raffia. New York: Alnap Co., Inc., 66 Reade Street, N.Y. 10007.

Denver Art Museum. Department of Art, Colorado.
Leaflet No. 5. "Pima Indian Close Coiled Basketry," 1930.
Leaflet No. 17. "Hopi Indian Basketry," 1931.
Leaflet No. 67. "Basketry Construction Technics," 1935.
Leaflet No. 68. "Basketry Decoration Technics," 1935.
Leaflets 83–84. "The Main Divisions of California Indian Basketry," 1937.
Leaflet No. 88. "Types of Southwestern Coiled Basketry," 1951.
Leaflets 99–100. "Southwestern Twined, Wicker, and Plaited Basketry," 1940.

Suppliers

The following supply sources are listed for your convenience. Materials offered and charges for samples and catalogs are subject to change without notice. No endorsement or responsibility is implied by the author. Price lists are free unless specified. The entry "basketry supplies" refers to reed, rattan, raffia, grasses, and similar materials, but dealers' inventories vary. For samples, a large self-addressed stamped envelope is suggested.

AAA Cordage Co., Inc. 3238 N. Clark Street Chicago, Ill. 60657	Twine, rope.	Samples: twines, $.50. ropes, $.50. twine and rope, $1.00.
Dick Blick Art Materials P. O. Box 1267 Galesburg, Ill. 61401	Assorted cords, yarns. Basketry supplies. Books.	Catalog.
Cane and Basket Supply Co. 1283 S. Cochran Avenue Los Angeles, Calif. 90019	Reed, rattan, raffia, fiber rush, seagrass, chair caning.	Samples and price list.
Carmel Valley Weavers Supply 1342 Camino Del Mar Del Mar, Calif. 92014	Wide variety imported yarns in all weights and textures. Unusual beads. Jute and sisal.	Samples: $.50.
CCM Arts and Crafts, Inc. 9520 Baltimore Avenue College Park, Md. 20740	Yarns, cords, basketry supplies. Books.	Catalog.
Colonial Woolen Mills, Inc. 6501 Barberton Avenue Cleveland, O. 44102	Assorted yarns.	Samples: $.50 Minimum order: $5.00.
Contessa Yarns P. O. Box 37 Lebanon, Conn. 06249	Assorted yarns.	Samples: $.25.
Craft Kaleidoscope 6551 Ferguson Street Broad Ripple Village Indianapolis, Ind. 46220	Wide variety cords, yarns and beads. Books. Dyes.	Send stamped self-addressed envelope for supply and price lists.

Craft Yarns of Rhode Island, Inc.
603 Mineral Spring Avenue
Pawtucket, R. I. 02862

Assorted yarns.

Samples: $.50

Creative Fibres, Inc.
1028 E. Juneau Avenue
Milwaukee, Wis. 53202

Large variety of cords, beads, misc. supplies. Books.

Catalog, price list: $1.00. Credited to first $5.00 order.

Creative Handweavers
P. O. Box 26480
Los Angeles, Calif. 90026

Tremendous variety of unusual yarns, cords, etc. Fleece, hair. Basketry supplies.

Wool and hair sample set: $1.00. Cotton and jute sample set: $1.00. Differs with yarns ordered. Wholesale prices on large amounts.

Dharma Trading Co.
P. O. Box 1288
Berkeley, Calif. 94701

Yarns, cordage, dyes. Books.

Samples: $.50. Minimum order: $5.00.

Earthworks
624 W. Willow Street
Chicago, Ill. 60614

Stoneware beads in 10 colors. Small and large holes and sizes.

Large bead samples: $1.00.

Earthy Endeavors
P. O. Box 817
Whittier, Calif. 90608

Ceramic, stoneware, and poreclain glazed and unglazed beads.

Minimum order: $1.50–$3.00. Wholesale information available.

El Mercado Importing Co.
9002 8th Avenue NE
Seattle, Wash. 98115

Natural Argentine and Mexican homespun sheepswool; natural, gray and dark brown.

Samples and price list: $.50.

Frederick J. Fawcett
129 South Street
Boston, Mass. 02111

Linen yarns. Large variety of textures and colors.

Samples: $1.00.

Freed Co.
Box 394
Albuquerque, N. M. 87103

Coral, glass beads, Indian-made wampum strands, turquoise, wool fleece, mohair and wool yarns, sheepskins, goatskins, leathers, wool carders, sea shells.

Free price lists and flyers.

Gooleni
11 Riverside Drive
Suite 5 VE
New York, N. Y. 10023

Seashells of many varieties.

Greentree Ranch Wools
Countryside Handweavers
163 N. Carter Lake Road
Loveland, Colo. 80537

Wide variety of fat yarns as well as traditional yarns.

Price list free.

Grey Owl Indian Craft Mfg. Co., Inc. 150-02 Beaver Road Jamaica, Queens, N. Y. 11433	American Indian craft supplies.	Catalog: $.25.
P. C. Herwig Co., Inc. Rt. 2, Box 140 Milaca, Minn. 56353	Linen yarns, sisal, jute, cotton, and rayon. Bells and beads.	Catalog and samples: $.50.
Hollywood Fancy Feather 512 S. Broadway Los Angeles, Calif. 90013	Assorted natural and dyed feathers.	Minimum order: $5.00.
International Handcraft and Supply 32 Hermosa Avenue Hermosa Beach, Calif. 90254	Yarns and cords including goathair, raw silk, leathers, beads.	Price list and samples: $1.00, deductible from first order. Minimum order: $5.00 plus tax and shipping costs.
Lamb's End 165 W. 9 Mile Road Ferndale, Mich. 48220	Yarns, feathers, beads, sea shells.	Yarn samples: $1.00. Minimum order: 1 lb. of fibers.
J. C. Larson Co. 7330 N. Clark Street Chicago, Ill. 60626	Yarns, cords. Basketry supplies. Books.	Catalog free.
Las Manos, Inc. 12215 Coit Road Dallas, Tex. 75230	Imported and domestic yarns, cords, beads.	Samples and price list: $.75. Minimum order: $10.00.
Lily Mills Co. Shelby, N. C. 28150	Yarns and threads.	Charge for samples.
Macramé and Weaving Supply Co. 63 E. Adams #403 Chicago, Ill. 60603	Yarns and supplies: beads, sea shells, feathers, bones.	Catalog free. Samples: $1.00.
The Mannings–Creative Crafts East Berlin, Penn. 17316	Wool, cotton, linen, and synthetic yarns; beads, cords. Books.	Catalog and samples: $.50. Minimum order: $5.00.
Naturalcraft 2199 Bancroft Way Berkeley, Calif. 94704	Beads, seashells, feathers, yarns and cordage. Basketry supplies.	Catalog and samples: $.50. Minimum order: $5.00.
Northwest Handcraft House 110 West Esplanade North Vancouver, B.C., Canada	Imported yarns, fleece, raw sisal, and manila, dyes, books.	Catalog: $.50.
Oregon Handspun Wool P. O. Box 132 Monroe, Ore. 97456	Handspun yarns.	Samples: $.50.

Pauline Paton,
Homespinner
134 Edgecumbe Road
Tauranga, New Zealand

N. Z. Fleece wool, spun one- and two-ply wools. Vegetable and chemical dyes.

Samples and price list.

Progress Feather Co.
657 W. Lake Street
Chicago, Ill.   60606

Assorted feathers. Pelts.

Free price list.
Minimum order: $15.00.
Wholesale only for quantity purchases.

Rip Neal Threads
9621 Seeley Lake Drive SW
Tacoma, Wash.   98499

Assorted threads and yarns. Beads, bells, books.

Price list free.

Sax Arts and Crafts
207 N. Milwaukee Street
Milwaukee, Wis.   53202

Assorted yarns. Basketry supplies. Books.

Catalog: $.50.

Tahki Imports, Ltd.
336 West End Avenue
New York, N. Y.   10023

Greek, Irish and Columbian handspun yarns.

Free catalog with information for ordering samples.

Three Gables Homecrafts
1825 Charleston Beach
Bremerton, Wash.   98310

Handcrafted glazed ceramic beads with large openings.

Free brochure with sample bead. Also wholesale to shops and schools.

Tuxedo Yarn and
Needlepoint
36–35 Main Street
Flushing, N. Y.   11354

Yarns and supplies. Beads.

Catalog free.

The Unique
21½ East Bijou
Colorado Springs, Colo.
80902

Imported yarns and threads.

Sample card: $1.00. Catalog of looms: $1.00. Complete portfolio of yarns and looms and catalogs: $8.00. Price list free.

Warp, Woof and Potpourri
514 N. Lake Avenue
Pasadena, Calif.   91101

Yarns, beads, dyes. Basketry supplies. Books.

Catalog and samples: $.50.

The Yarn Depot, Inc.
545 Sutter Street
San Francisco, Calif.
94102

Assorted yarns, beads. Basketry supplies. Books.

Samples: $.50 to $1.50. Bimonthly samples club.

The Yarn Loft
Upstairs, 1442 Camino
Del Mar
Del Mar, Calif.   92014

Fibers for all crafts. Metallic yarns. Basketry supplies.

Catalog: $1.00.

Yarn Primitives
P. O. Box 1013
Weston, Conn.   06880

Handspun yarns from Greece, Ecuador, Peru, Bolivia, India, and Haiti. Wools, goat hair, cotton blends.

Catalog: $2.00.
Samples: $2.00.

Index